COASTLINE
An Anthology
of the Welsh Coast

Coastline

An Anthology of the Welsh Coast

Compiled by
Dewi Roberts

Foreword by
Mike Parker

Published with the financial support
of the Welsh Books Council.

ISBN: 1-84527-022-3

Cover design: Sian Parri
Cover illustration: Rob Piercy
Maps: Ken Gruffydd

Published in 2005
by Gwasg Carreg Gwalch, 12 Iard yr Orsaf,
Llanrwst, Wales LL26 0EH
✆ *01492 642031* 📠 *01492 641502*
✆ *books@carreg-gwalch.co.uk   Website: www.carreg-gwalch.co.uk*

Contents

7

Foreword

Perhaps more than any other country in these islands, the image of Wales, both to itself and the world, is largely defined by its natural landscape. With four-fifths of the country's landmass being upland, small wonder that it is mainly the mountains, hills and valleys that offer themselves most readily as images of Wales and Welshness. Countless bards, writers, artists and photographers have been inspired by Wales' magnificent countryside and there is, it seems, an insatiable hunger amongst both Welsh people and visitors for literature and art rooted in the soil and rock of Cymru.

The no less magnificent Welsh coast, however, seems to get rather overlooked. Aside from the trappings of the major holiday resorts, we see but a fraction of the influence of the sea on our national consciousness. This anthology goes some small way to redressing the balance, and not before time. The range of writers – including Hilaire Belloc, Samuel Taylor Coleridge, John Betjeman, Jonathan Swift, Paul Theroux, William Condry, Bobi Jones, Gwyn Thomas, Francis Kilvert and the Thomases R.S. and Dylan – is as impressive and eclectic as you'd hope, spanning the centuries from the ninth to the twenty-first.

Perhaps the coast's lower profile in our consciousness has something to do with the fact that, in Wales as much as anywhere, it is something of a separate country. Whereas most hill farmers and inland dwellers would, until really quite recently, seldom have travelled much beyond their *milltir sgwar*, the ports and harbours were full of sea captains and crew who had sailed to all corners of the globe, giving the towns and villages of the sea a curious cosmopolitanism. As an elderly resident of New Quay put it to me 'no-one here had been to Birmingham, but many had seen Buenos Aires'. Add to that the very real – and very regular – spectre of death and tragedy hanging over communities locked in an umbilical relationship with the sea, and it's clear how distinct and discrete the coastal identity can be. These legacies are still to be seen today and chime through many of the pieces in this book.

According to the Ordnance Survey, the coastline of Wales totals 1317.26 miles, or 1680.31 miles – further than Cardiff to Athens or Moscow – if you include all the offshore islands. Within those 1680 miles, the variety of landscapes is quite breathtaking, whether in the wild, seabird-swirling cliffs of Ynys Môn, Ceredigion and Pembrokeshire, the belching heavy industry of Flintshire and Swansea Bay or the eerie, misty flatlands of Meirionnydd, the Gwent Levels and northern Gower. I am lucky enough to have seen most of it from the sea, after presenting two series of television programmes (*Coast to Coast* for ITV Wales) sailing around the Welsh coast in different vessels, from schooners to ketches, a lavish gin palace to a rusty four hundred ton sand dredger.

So much in this book took me straight back to those two recent summers spent sailing rather gracelessly around Wales. For a confirmed landlubber like me, the first lesson was in learning to respect the sea's mighty power. Here, schedules and diaries count for nothing. Everything was subordinate to the weather conditions, the tides and the swell, and, even then, things can go horribly wrong. I winced at Hilaire Belloc's memory of Swnt Enlli (Bardsey Sound) and its 'hell of white water and noise', for it was precisely there, one of the most dangerous stretches of sea on the entire British coast, that we got into terrible trouble and ended up having to be rescued. 'All the waters of the world and all its winds / Roar blazing on this little coast', states Leslie Norris. Don't I know it.

The timelessness of the sea means that we slip between the worlds, and between the past, present and future, so

11

much more readily on the coast. For many of us, the very tang of salty air can whisk us back to childhood in an instant, whether to crabbing amongst the rockpools, never-ending days of sun and sand or stolen kisses behind the ice cream parlour, and all of it drenched in that bright, bluey, eternal light. Time moves differently where earth meets sea; it has, as Dylan Thomas says of Laugharne, a 'sane disregard for haste'. People often talk of the *mañana* attitude of Spain, or even Ireland, but it's something I've grasped joyfully in Wales too, none more so than in the quirky communities of the seaside.

Talking of Dylan Thomas, I'm very pleased indeed to see that Dewi Roberts has firmly nailed his colours to the mast as regards the location of Thomas' masterpiece, *Under Milk Wood*. He places some text for *Milk Wood*'s precursor, a short story called *Quite Early One Morning*, in Laugharne, Carmarthenshire, the town in which Thomas and his family lived for many years and which refuses to countenance that anywhere else could have inspired the author in his best-known work. Not so. In this collection, the text of *Under Milk Wood* is clearly placed at New Quay, Ceredigion, where the Thomases lived for a short, but turbulent, period during the Second World War. It's a decision that will not please the good people of Laugharne, a wonderfully odd town for sure, but nowhere near as Llaregub as prim-yet-priapic little New Quay.

Any country with a coastline has its tales of lost lands and submerged cities, and it's no surprise that Wales – a nation than can spin a good yarn out of thin air – is particularly strong in this department. Here we learn of the Cantre'r Gwaelod, the lost plain of sixteen golden cities in Cardigan Bay, but also think of the ghosts of Aberffraw, the spirits of the sunken city of Llys Helig near Penmaenmawr and the twenty thousand saints who coughed their last after the hellish sea journey over to Ynys Enlli, that whale-shaped

12

droplet of land that, perhaps more than anywhere, crystallises and symbolises the Welsh relationship with its ocean. Not that we're allowed to get too lachrymose or sentimental here – just read Harri Webb's fantastically scabrous poem about Enlli and its oft-spun place in the Welsh pantheon of glory.

To every one of us, the sea, and the communities straggled perilously along its fringe, conjures up a host of different images and feelings. This collection takes that huge variety and writes it even larger, through different eyes in very many different ages. The fisherman, the artist, the tourist, the farmer, the shipbuilder, the master mariner, the soldier, the sailor, the publican, the poet and the pisshead all mix on this very edge of life, on the border between the safe and the perilous. A distant ocean horizon – especially, as in most of Wales, when it is zapped by the daily splendour of a sunset – encourages lofty thoughts and ambition, coupled with a rare sense of perspective and humility. The coast is a place that inspires some of the best work of any artist or writer. This glorious collection only proves that point.

Mike Parker

Introduction

The *sea* and the communities which are situated along its periphery possess a singular history and mythology. The legend of Llys Helig and Cantre'r Gwaelod are both concerned with events which occurred in lands beneath the sea at some very ancient period.

Although there are accounts of these and other mythical events in these pages there are also at least a certain number of purely historical items. These cover the last invasion of Wales in 1797, the Anglesey wreckers of the eighteenth century and the disaster which befell the 'Royal Charter'. However the main emphasis of the selection is literary and in over seventy poems and over forty prose extracts the reader is taken on a journey around the Welsh coast from the Dee Estuary in the north east to the Severn Estuary in the south east. It is the sense of place which is the dominant motif and this includes not only regions, towns and villages but also a number of the islands which lie off the coast.

The work of both Welsh writers in English and Welsh language writers in translation is represented including Dylan Thomas, R.S. Thomas, Vernon Watkins, Leslie Norris, Dannie Abse, Gillian Clarke, Sian James and Peter Finch. Welsh language poets on board include Bobi Jones, Cynan and R. Gerallt Jones. English writers who have written about Wales and her coast are numerous and readers will encounter a fairly small number of these here, they include Dickens, Arnold Bennett, John Betjeman, Robert Graves and Hilaire Belloc.

The writer's eye is one which is capable of creating a fresh perspective on both the many moods of the sea as well as the distinctive character of each of the communities included.

Dewi Roberts

Acknowledgements

We wish to thank the following publishers, agents, authors and other owners of copyright for granting us permission to include the items below in these pages:

'The Sea', 'Abersoch' and 'Schoonerman' from *Collected Poems* by R.S. Thomas, reprinted by permission of J.M. Dent, a division of the Orion Publishing Group.

'A Short History of the North Wales Coast', 'Sunny Prestatyn' and 'In Port Talbot' from *North and South* (Seren 2002).

Lloyd Jones: two extracts from *Mr Vogel* (Seren 2004).

Steve Griffiths: 'Misrule Tywyn 1990' from *Selected Poems* (Seren 1993).

Catherine Fisher: 'Incident at Conwy' from *The Unexplored Ocean* (Seren 1994).

Frances Sackett: 'Change of weather at Conwy' from *The Hand Glass*. (Seren 1996).

Christine Evans: 'Enlli' from *Selected Poems* (Seren 2004).

Duncan Bush: *The Sea, The Sea* from 'Poetry Wales: 25 years' edited by Cary Archard (Seren 1997) and 'Ramsay Island' from *The Hook* (Seren 1997).

Jean Earle: 'Solva Harbour' from *Visiting Light* (Poetry Wales Press 1987).

Ruth Bidgood: 'Leaving the Beach' and 'Llansteffan' from *Singing to Wolves* (Seren 2000).

Don Rogers: 'Burry Holm' from *Multiverse* (Seren 2000).

Peter Finch: 'Severn Estuary ABC' from *Poems for Ghosts* (Seren 1991) and an extract from *Real Cardiff* (Seren 2000).

Robert Minhinnick: 'Dock' from *The Dinosaur Park* (Poetry Wales Press 1985).

Gwasg Carreg Gwalch for 'A Family of Resorts' from *Coast to Coast* by Mike Parker (2004).

Tony Connor for 'Above Penmaenmawr'.

Sally Roberts Jones for 'Bangor Pier' from *Turning Away*.

Alice Thomas Ellis: 'Llyn Helig' from *A Welsh Childhood*.

Peter Gruffydd: Slate Quarry – Felinheli which appeared in *The Shivering Seed* (Chatto and Windus).

Huw Jones: 'Britain's Treasure Island' by permission of the poet.

Jim Perrin 'On Carmel Head' from *Spirits of Peace* © Gomer: 1997.

Gwyn Thomas: 'Crossing a Shore' translated by Tony Conran by permission of the author.

Robert Graves: *'Welsh Incident'* by permission of Carcanet.

Paul Henry: 'Welsh Incident' from *'The Bread Thief* (Seren 1998).

Cynan: 'Aberdaron' from *'Twentieth Century Welsh Poetry* translated and edited by Joseph P. Clancy (Gomer 1982).

(2) extract from *The Kingdom by the Sea* by Paul Theroux (Hamish Hamilton: 1983) © Paul Theroux.

Roland Mathias for his poem 'Freshwater West'. The Estate of R.G. Prys Jones for 'St Govan'.

John Powell Ward: 'Port Eynon' originally appeared in *Roundyhouse*.

The extract from Robert Nisbet's short story *Jam Jars of Seaweed and Dreams of Love* appeared in 'Downtrain' which was published by Parthian in 2004.

'Expedition Skomer' appear by permission of Raymond Garlick.

'Caldy' from *Some Lovely Islands* by Leslie Thomas appears with the consent of the author.

'A Childhood in Tenby' from *Chiascuro* by Augustas John appears by permission of David Higham Associates.

Vernon Watkins: 'Ode to Swansea' appear by kind permission of Mrs Gwen Watkins.

Peter Read's poem 'Swansea Bay' appears by permission of the poet.

Dannie Abse: 'By Ogmore by Sea This August Evening' appears by permission of the poet.

Idris Davies: 'Let's go to Barry Island, Maggie fach' and 'Tiger Bay' appear with the permission of the Estate of Idris Davies.

Anthony Bailey: the extract from *A Walk through Wales* (Cape 1992) appears with the permission of the author.

Jan Morris: Two extracts from *Wales: Epic Views of a Small Country* (Viking 1998) appear with the permission of the author © Jan Morris.

Alison Bielkski: 'Wreck of a Bristol trader' is published with the consent of the poet.

The extract from *Ennal's Point* (Penguin 1977) appears here with the consent of the Estate of Alan Richards.

John Tripp: 'At Bosherston Ponds' appears with the consent of the Estate of John Tripp.

Gillian Clarke: 'Heron at Port Talbot' from *Collected Poems* (Carcanet).

Richard Poole: 'Interlude at Traeth Bychan' appeared in *An Anglesey Anthology* edited by Dewi Roberts (Gwasg Carreg Gwalch 1999) and 'Seasky' in *Autobiographies and Explorations* (Headland 1994).

Richard Rhydderch: an extract from his short story 'A Visit to the Bay' which originally appeared in *Planet* Number 67 Oct/Nov. 2004.

Stephen Knight: 'The End of the Pier'. Our thanks to the author for allowing us to reprint his poem which originally appeared in *Poetry Wales* Volume 34/0 (1999).

Alan Perry: 'Snaps at Gower, 1933' by permission of the poet.

Both Tony Conran's 'Trippers at Aberffraw' and his translation of the anonymous 'Ode to Tenby' appear here by permission of the poet.

Tony Curtis: 'Pwllcrochan' from *Selected Poems*, Poetry Wales Press 1987.

The Felix de Wolfe Agency for two extracts from *The Welsh Eye* by Gwyn Thomas (Hutchinson 1964).

R.M. Lockley's *The Island* – an extract from this title reproduced with the permission of Andre Deutch.

Catherine Fisher: sequence from 'Estuary Poems' from *Altered States* (Seren 1997).

Erica Woof: extract from *Mud Puppy* by courtesy of The Women's Press 2002.

Cynan: 'Abedaron' from *Twentieth Century Welsh Poems* edited and translated by Joseph P. Clancy (Gomer 1982)

It has not proved possible to contact all owners of copyright and we apologise for any omissions from the above list.

The Sea

They wash their hands in it.
The salt turns to soap
In their hands. Wearing it
At their wrists, they make
Of it; it runs in beads
On their jackets. A child's
Plaything? It has hard whips
That it cracks, and knuckles
To pummel you. It scrubs
And scours; it chews rocks
To sand; its embraces
Leave you without breath. Mostly
It is a stomach, where bones,
Wrecks, continents are digested.

R.S. Thomas

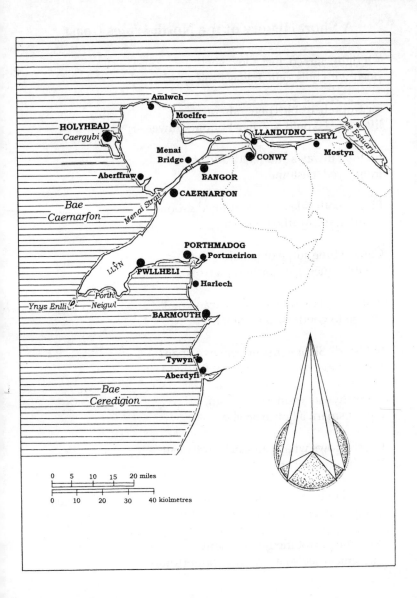

Amlwch
Moelfre
HOLYHEAD
Caergybi
LLANDUDNO
RHYL
Dee Estuary
Menai
Bridge
CONWY
Mostyn
Aberffraw
BANGOR
CAERNARFON
Bae Caernarfon
Menai Strait
LLŶN
PORTHMADOG
Portmeirion
PWLLHELI
Harlech
Porth Neigwl
Ynys Enlli
BARMOUTH
Tywyn
Aberdyfi
Bae Ceredigion

0   5   10   15   20 miles
0   10   20   30   40 kiolmetres

A Short History of the North Wales Coast

All right, agreed, just a low shelf
piled with hills. Still, it was itself –

incomprehensible come rain or war,
life folded, you'd say, in a bottom drawer –

till the railway's sudden drum
thundered 'customers'.

Bingo. Both sides across stunned ground
snuffled like truffle hounds.

Came a blue surge of matelots,
quaintesques, glee parties, pierrots,

and the Palace saw a real African kraal
stretch to gondolas on a canal

St David? Slept in magic groves a span?
Would have sold out, *Dave the Fasting Man.*

Here anyway in an early photo,
advert smart, a house on show

foreshadows what's all spick and spent.
It is the ghost of crisis present:

on her lawn like a Welcome mat,
a lady addresses a caged bird. Just that.

With the parrot though, so many
ears unlearned so much from opportunity

that tongues licked brandnew speech.
And all changed. Like that. It's teaching

time at Bagíllt where our lady misrule
has started up the Parrot School.

John Davies

A View From The Train

At Mostyn the landscape acquired a definite character,
unfolding more beautifully and richly, the further our train
advanced; indeed, here it reveals in advance what the
traveller can expect from the Welsh highlands, where the
footpath, like the railway, leads from surprise to surprise
between sea and mountain. On our left lay a large
luxuriantly green oak wood, from the midst of which on a
jutting rock rose a castle looking most picturesque with its
white walls in such a lovely setting. Then the view extended
out to the open sea, rolling here between the Welsh shore
and the coasts of Ireland. I had never made such a journey in
my life before; for even the Belgian train from Verviers to
Liege, which had charmed me so much, I cannot compare
with this. There as here you have the charming green
landscape and the mountains, powerfully and picturesquely
grouped; but in Wales there is also the sea, and always so
close that you think the waves must be lapping the wheels
of the engine. Beside the sea the mountains extended for a
while like steep grey masses of rock, to which the evening
twilight lent a wonderfully gentle shade approaching violet.
But then suddenly, at Rhyl, a wide valley opened out, the

widening prospect affording even greater pleasure to the soul of the beholder. The bluish mountains bounded it in a vast circle, one towering above the other and only sparsely wooded here and there, but appearing inhabited with many scattered individual buildings as one approached them nearer. The scenes and view alternated swiftly; now the sea was visible, now it disappeared for a time. But then at Abergele it lay before us in its full extent, with ships in the sunset, and the roaring and breaking of its waves announcing that the tide had returned; and though during the ebb the sea is somewhat dreamy or even dead, with the fuller beat of its flood tide it awakens life and the joy of living, and as this change occurs several times a day before the eyes of the beholder, always affecting the spirit through the senses, perhaps this is the great and healing magic which contemplative natures always receive from it. Here a most impressive landscape confronts the lively waves, forming a sharply marked contrast to the endless sheet of water, which on so many other shores loses itself secretly in the sand. On a fragrantly wooded line of hills lies a little town, and high above, in a green wooded ravine, stately castle buildings with towers and battlements in a semicircle, and the sea roaring below the cliffs. Here the train had to work its way several times through the massive coastal cliffs, every time causing great surprise as we suddenly emerged from minutes in the darkness of one of these tunnels to see the shoreless sea close before us, so close indeed as to think that the whole train must plunge down into it.

Julius Rodenberg (1831-1914): An Autumn In Wales, translated and edited by William Linnell

The Sands of Dee

'0 Mary, go and call the cattle home,
   And call the cattle home,
   And call the cattle home,
   Across the sands of Dee.'
The western wind was wild and dark with foam,
   And all alone went she.

The western tide crept up along the sand,
   And o'er and o'er the hand,
   And round and round the sand,
   As far as eye could see.
The rolling mist came down and hid the land:
   And never home came she.

'0 is it weed or fish or floating hair –
   A tress of golden hair,
   A drowned maiden's hair,
   Above the nets at sea?'
Was never salmon yet that shone so fair
   Among the stakes of Dee.

They row'd her in across the rolling foam,
   The cruel crawling foam,
   The cruel hungry foam,
   To her grave beside the sea.
But still the boatmen hear her call the cattle home,
   Across the sands of Dee.

Charles Kingsley (1819-1875)

An Estuary View

Seven o'clock in the morning. Standing on top of the old lime kiln, Richard Bloyd glanced at his wrist-watch, held it close to his ear, and then plunged his hands once more deep into his overcoat pockets. It was a fine morning, but still chilly. Across the water he saw the Wirral emerge from the early morning mist; become once more a solid and substantial rich-green sea-girt land, speckled with red-roofed houses. The tide was out and down the estuary the mud flats gleamed in the oblique rays of the sun like the backs of enormous slugs resting in the low water. Down below on the water's edge the colliery's gaunt cranes emerged from a pall of mist and smoke, in its small harbour a dirty steamer blew its fog-horn into the silence, and after the silence was broken the day awoke. A train raced urgently across the coastal plain, as though all consideration was over, all decisions made, and the execution of plans begun.

Emyr Humphreys: The Little Kingdom (1946)

Prestatyn

They who through dirt and wet can wade
Without a clog or patten
May share the fate of many a maid
That lives at poor Prestatyn.

But one who wants a goose to eat,
Or famous hog to fatten;
Will find none such on any coast
As ours of poor Prestatyn.

Here none are seen of Bond Street beaux,
Or belles in silk and satin;
But you may save your own best clothes
By living at Prestatyn.

No conversation with wise men,
Expert in Greek and Latin;
But you may use a book or pen,
At pitiful Prestatyn.

If then you languish with ennui,
And hope begins to flatten;
Come, bathe in our bold Irish Sea
That roars about Prestatyn.

Here cloudless suns will set and rise
At Vespers and at Matin;
And those whose hearts such sights do prize
Will value poor Prestatyn.

For me, though there's no breadth nor length
Nor room to swing a cat in,
When I am distressed for health or strength
Pray send me to Prestatyn.

Hesta Thrale (later Piozzi) (1741-1821)

Sunny Prestatyn

Each day I see them carefully grow old and feed
        behind that glass, those plants,
in an aquarium's stillness — saw at first their need
        for aloneness like a niche.
It is not a need. Lured by sun-crossed memories
        of August, most have retired
from industrial towns at last to find the sea
        sucked out of reach.

They have left the wet streets that flow
        on northern towns like tides,
those separately secret worlds that tow
        forever in their wake
lives bound by the going and returning they inhabit,
        for this quiet place
where silent mornings on the daylight hours sit.
        Here no tide will break.

Some watch the sand, the blank sea stretching out, going
        endlessly nowhere.
Past bungalows, an empty paper bag goes yachting
        down the empty Street.
Cars pass; seagulls stream on white safaris to the sea.
        Like their bungalows,
the old here are detached, with no shared memory
        to sift or curse or greet.

And if they had known of this, would they have stayed
   where home and friends
still were, where the family was once, and made
   the most of their discharge?
Anywhere, lack of interest, change and age itself condemn
   them, left on some beach
or trapped in tanks. We are accused of them
   and they are us writ large.

John Davies: 'At The Edge Of Town'
© Gomer 1981

Not For Cold Print

In the evening, out of a sense of duty, I took a bus and went
to see Rhyl. Wild horses shall not drag from me a full
account of that horror; 'neither wild 'orses, nor blood 'orses,
nor race 'orses, nor cart 'orses, nor Suffolk punches' – in the
cumulative phrase of Mary Webb's Andrew Vesson. What I
think of Rhyl is not for cold print; it belongs to flaming
forbidden words which would scorch this page. But I will
say this: that if one were to entrust the architecture of an
important town to a committee formed from representatives
of the designers of fancy cakes, dolls' houses, and toy Swiss
chalets, and from the artists who paint the pictures on
crackers and chocolate-box lids, with power to co-opt from
the ranks of the worst jerry-builders in the country, and the
worst sign-writers in the world, then the result would be a
flattering imitation of the sea-front at Rhyl. The whole town
resembles a cheap bazaar; indeed, its appearance of
impermanence is the most pleasing thing about it. The few
good buildings which it possesses seem to rise up out of a

chaos of pink sugar-rock, which mocks them shamefully. Indeed, my impression of Rhyl, now six weeks old, is that it achieves an effect of staggering baroque by the admixture of bad buildings and monstrous sticks of this red and yellow stuff. But really Rhyl is indescribable; it is like the wrath of God.

John Moore (1907-1967): Tramping Through Wales

The Blackpool of North Wales

Rhyl is the Blackpool of North Wales, a typical British seaside resort dripping with ice cream, hot dogs and candy floss, bingo halls and flashing bauble-rooms full of coin-gulping bandits and those impossible machines with a grab which invite you to fish for a fluffy toy and never, ever, give you one. I have never heard of anyone in the entire history of seaside resorts who has succeeded in prising a single useless teddy from those machines. Rhyl is where millions of people belonging to the old working classes went on holiday before Europe was discovered. Personally I quite like Rhyl's jaded charms, but others have been less kind.

On my trek I had walked past the Alex, as the hospital is known locally. It lies isolated at the eastern end of the prom, a reminder, like some of the large Victorian houses nearby, of better days, when four railway tracks teeming with steam trains brought the first wave of pleasure-seekers into Wales. Wild Bill Hickok brought his touring Buffalo Bill's Wild West Show here in a convoy of trains, and the redoubtable Arthur Cheetham introduced moving pictures, phrenology and water electrolysis to heal those with enough time and money. It was that sort of age.

Lloyd Jones: Mr Vogel (2004)

Jellyfish (Marine Lake, Rhyl)

The water is milky with *medusae*.
A seminal gathering of thousands
Pulsates, thrusts, throbs beneath the surface
Spasm after spasm after spasm.
A flotilla of free floating
Silken parachutes drifts, swirls.
Translucent, they mushroom gently in the swell
Fronds tangle and trail.

Formation dancers in this aquatic palais
Undulate, sway
Skirts ballooning at each turn.
Parisienne artistes Can-can
Wanton, wild, kick high
Choreography inspired.
Slavonic steps, gossamer gowns
Show a stately
Petticoat polonaise.

Apparitions quiver tremulous
Into reality
As, back home, I scan *First Aid in English*,
Group Terms Or Collections,
For the word on the tip of my memory.

A clowder of cats, a kindle of kittens
A siege of herons, a wisp of snipe.
A smuck of jellyfish.

Gene Groves

Misrule, Towyn, 1990

With a clatter, the sea pushes
its tongue through the letterbox.
It does not empty or relieve itself.
The Axminster rises towards the ceiling,
passing a barometer half way up.

This is my home and I'm having it back
from the sea: swilling up to the front room sill
and window-frame, newly reglossed
in duck-egg blue,
fourteen years of marriage.
Grateful to find there are knickers
intact on the top shelf: one pair fresh
as rising dough on the hearth
and I'm ready to meet my maker.

Hers is a small house
in a silent gallery of snow,
in a plastic capsule won from a cracker,
broken soon: a hermit crab
darts below the swirling fall of sand
among the surging levities of beach-plastic
and the shoes that feel life returning
in the bedroom.

The rattle of shingle
is uniform and triumphant
across the kitchen floors of Towyn.

On a roof anchored uncertainly with planks,
there were ovals of grey ice
on blue plastic sheeting
like lakes from a plane in blue mountains
as I lean down from an early meal.

Over his muesli, my son asks
if it was like this in Atlantis,
a little water
riding together suddenly
over the flat of his hand
as he lowers it in the bath,
knocking the houses over, like this.

I must have been twelve or thereabouts
when I pored through the atlas,
speculating what would be left of the uplands

if the sea reached six hundred feet,
recording it all meticulously
as the sea blustered
not far from the door:

the West Siberian Plain,
the basin of the Ganges and the Brahmaputra,

the Fens, the North European Plain,
most of Cheshire
was it the fury of clouds I wanted
or simply disorder,
was it a sad end,

was it a just desert
or the little death
that sets a story in motion?
The strong winds rage along the isobars
and people begin not to notice
how it plucks and tears at awnings,
raging at bars,
perhaps more than it did before.
On the way to work,
I noticed how the buildings
loitered in the street,
how I could have stopped
and watched anything happen:

it was a sharp cold day,
people ran to the river bank
as a shack approached
and floated slowly past:
at the open back a boy and a small girl,
between them a dog with its back to the water,
the boy taking pulls of a cigarette,
the girl holding the tip of the dog's tail
between her fingers in the same way,
pale and very concentrated.
We were left gawping.

We felt our ways
upstream and down
for something familiar.

But now you cannot retreat as far as the sea
you belong to
because it will come for you.

Steve Griffiths: 'Selected Poems'
© Seren

The Walking Stick

Abergele is a large village on the sea coast. Walking on the sea sands I was surprised to see a number of fine women bathing promiscuously with men and boys perfectly naked! Doubtless, the citadels of their chastity are so impregnably strong that they need not the ornamental outworks of modesty. But seriously speaking, where sexual distinctions are least observed men and women live together in the greatest purity. Concealment sets the imagination a working . . . Just before I quitted Cambridge I met a countryman with a strange walking stick, five feet in length. I eagerly bought it and a most faithful servant it has proved to be. *My* sudden affection for it has mellowed into settled friendship. On the morning of our leaving Abergele just before our final departure I looked for the stick in the place where I had left it overnight. It was gone! I alarmed the house. No one knew anything of it. In the flurry of anxiety I sent for the crier of the town and gave him the following to cry about the town and on the beach, which he did with a gravity for which I am indebted to his stupidity.

'Missing from the Bee Inn, Abergele, a curious walking stick. On one side it displays the head of an eagle . . . On the other side is the portrait of the owner in wood work . . . If any gentleman or lady has fallen in love with the above described stick and secretly carried it off, he or she is hearby earnestly admonished to conquer a passion, the continuence of which must prove fatal to his or her honesty; and if the said stick has slipped into such gentlemans or ladies hands through inadvertence, he, or she, is required to rectify the mistake with all convenient speed. God save the King.'

Abergele is a fashionable Welsh watering place and so singular a proclamation excited no small crowd on the beach, among the rest a lame old gentleman in whose hands I espied my stick. The old gent, who lodged at our inn, felt

great confusion, and walked homeward, the solemn crier
before him, and a various cavalcade behind . . . He made his
lameness an apology for borrowing my stick . . . Thus it
ended . . .

Samuel Taylor Coleridge (1772-1834):
included in 'A Pedestrian Tour of North Wales',
edited by William Tydeman and Alun R. Jones

Swimming in the Restless Sea

. . . at last I could smell the sea, and the road curled
westward. I was able to leave it now, and to walk along the
shore. Far in front of me I could see Colwyn Bay; but here I
was quite alone with the sad crying of the gulls, the
whistling of the flocks of sandpiper, and the lovely restless
surge of the sea.

I took off my clothes, and ran into it till I was waist-deep;
and then I plunged in and swam under water till I came up
gasping and choking, and shaking myself because of its
delicious coldness. Out and out I swam into the blue gleam
of it, till all tiredness was forgotten, love and philosophy
and books and the making of books, and the whole of life
was no more than the lapping of the ripples and a sweet
tingling.

When I had had enough I swam back and lay naked in
the sun, thinking of nothing at all, and listening to the swish
of the little waves that came up so regularly and broke
themselves on the pebbles. Them I could understand
without thinking, for the sea is as restless as I am, never still
and never at peace for long, always seeking something more

than it has, something which it knows it can never have, in all the long years.

John Moore (1907-1967): Tramping Through Wales

A Family of Resorts

From the sea, the first striking thing to notice was just how developed the coastal strip is here. Prestatyn, Rhyl, Kinmel Bay, Towyn, Abergele, Llanddulas, Colwyn Bay and Rhos-on-Sea all merge into one another in a seamless, uninterrupted sprawl, some sixteen miles long. It was something of a relief to see nature reassert itself as we approached the headland of the Little Orme. This ancient limestone crag, and its bigger brother the Great Orme, perfectly frame the seaside resort of Llandudno that we could just see peeping around the corner. But there was an unexpected diversion in the shape of a school of dolphins playing out at sea. Scott turned us round and we headed off to see them.

Words cannot do justice to the experience of having a load of dolphins showing off around you. They were jumping either side of the boat and evidently playing with us, and loving every single second. It was quite breathtaking. There really is something about these graceful creatures. I'm as cynical as anyone, but after a few minutes of this, it was all I could do to stop myself stripping off, leaping in and having the proverbial mystical experience. After the dolphins had moved on, we started to steer back towards Llandudno, all of us with daft, soppy grins spread across our faces.

Every travel writer who's ever visited Llandudno has

come away at least reasonably impressed by the unity and scale of the town's Regency architecture. Even Bill Bryson, in his often hilarious *Notes from a Small Island*, took a break from his all too predictable pops at the northern Wales coastline to admit that Llandudno was 'truly a fine and handsome place'. It's even better from a boat. Instead of approaching the town past B&Q superstores and miles of thirties semis, and then spending forty minutes driving around in circles looking for a parking space, all of which kind of dilutes the impact of the place, we just rounded a corner and – bang! – there it was, laid out like an elegant Merchant Ivory film set. My instant reaction was of the stark contrast with Colwyn Bay, which hides from its own seafront. None of that malarkey with Llandudno. The whole town drapes itself with unabashed pride around the gentle curve of the bay, sandwiched with perfect precision between the dual hummocks of the Ormes, Great and Little.

If the resorts of northern Wales were a family, Prestatyn would be a quite likeable, but rather dull, cousin, Rhyl a beered-up brother who you worry might be nicking cars and Colwyn Bay the ageing auntie who lost her looks years back. But the biggest character in the clan is Great Uncle Llandudno, the elegant old chap who might be a bit threadbare in places if you look a little too closely, but who can still swagger with a certain bygone panache. From his position spread languidly around the bay beneath the Great Orme, Great Uncle Llandudno looks along – and it has to be said, looks down on – the rest of his family with a barely disguised shudder of horror.

Mike Parker: Coast To Coast (2004)

At the Eisteddfod

The summer before last I spent some weeks at Llandudno, on the Welsh coast. The best lodging-houses at Llandudno look eastward, towards Liverpool; and from that Saxon hive swarms are incessantly issuing, crossing the bay, and taking possession of the beach and the lodging-houses. Guarded by the Great and Little Orme's Head, and alive with the Saxon invaders from Liverpool, the eastern bay is an attractive point of interest, and many visitors to Llandudno never contemplate anything else. But, putting aside the charm of the Liverpool steamboats, perhaps the view, on this side, a little dissatisfies one after a while; the horizon wants mystery, the sea wants beauty, the coast wants verdure, and has a too bare austereness and aridity. At last one turns round and looks westward. Everything is changed. Over the mouth of the Conway and its sands is the eternal softness and mild light of the west; the low line of the mystic Anglesey, and the precipitous Penmaenmawr, and the great group of Carnedd Llewelyn and Carnedd David and their brethren fading away, hill behind hill, in an aerial haze, make the horizon; between the foot of Penmaenmawr and the bending coast of Anglesey, the sea, a silver stream, disappears one knows not whither. On this side Wales – Wales, where the past still lives, where every place has its tradition, every name its poetry, and where the people, the genuine people, still knows this past, this tradition, this poetry, and lives with it, and clings to it; while, alas, the prosperous Saxon on the other side, the invader from Liverpool and Birkenhead, has long ago forgotten his.

But the Celtic genius was just then preparing, in Llandudno, to have its hour of revival. Workmen were busy in putting up a large tent-like wooden building, which attracted the eye of every newcomer, and which my little boys believed (their wish, no doubt, being father to their belief) to be a circus. It turned out, however, to be no circus (for Castor and Pollux) but a temple for Apollo and the Muses. It was the place where the Eisteddfod, or Bardic Congress of Wales, was about to be held; a meeting which has for its object (I quote the words of its promoters) 'the diffusion of useful knowledge, the eliciting of native talent, and the cherishing of love of home and honourable fame by the cultivation of poetry, music and art.' My little boys were disappointed; but I, whose circus days are over, I, who have a professional interest in poetry, and who, also, hating all one-sidedness and oppression, wish nothing better than that the Celtic genius should be able to show itself to the world and to make its voice heard, was delighted. I took my ticket, and waited impatiently for the day of opening. The day came, an unfortunate one; storms of wind, clouds of dust, an angry, dirty sea. The Saxons who arrived by the Liverpool steamers looked miserable; even the Welsh who arrived by land – whether they were discomposed by the bad morning, or by the monstrous and crushing tax which the London and North-Western Railway Company levies on all whom it transports across those four miles of marshy peninsula between Conway and Llandudno – did not look happy. First we went to the Gorsedd, or preliminary congress for conferring the degree of bard. The Gorsedd was held in the open air, at the windy corner of a street, and the morning was not favourable to open-air solemnities. The Welsh, too, share, it seems to me, with their Saxon invaders, an inaptitude for show and spectacle. Show and spectacle are better managed by the Latin race, and those whom it has moulded; the Welsh, like us, are a little awkward and resourceless in the organisation of a festival. The presiding genius of the mystic circle, in our hideous nineteenth-century costume relieved only by a green scarf, the wind drowning his voice and the dust powdering his whiskers, looked thoroughly wretched; so did the aspirants for bardic honours; and I believe, after about an hour of it, we all of us, as we stood shivering round the sacred stones, began half to wish for the Druid's sacrificial knife to end our sufferings.

Mathew Arnold (1822-1888):
On the Study of Celtic Literature

Denry's Holiday

Ruth chose Llandudno, Llandudno being more stylish than either Rhyl or Blackpool, and not dearer. Ruth and Nellie had a double room in a boarding-house, No. 26 St Asaph's Road (off the Marine Parade), and Denry had a small single room in another boarding-house, No. 28 St Asaph's Road. The ideal could scarcely have been approached more nearly.

Denry had never seen the sea before. As, in his gayest clothes, he strolled along the esplanade or on the pier between those two girls in their gayest clothes, and mingled with the immense crowd of pleasure-seekers and money-spenders, he was undoubtedly much impressed by the beauty and grandeur of the sea. But what impressed him far more than the beauty and grandeur of the sea was the field for profitable commercial enterprise which a place like Llandudno presented. He had not only his first vision of the sea, but his first genuine vision of the possibilities of amassing wealth by honest ingenuity. On the morning after his arrival he went out for a walk and lost himself near the Great Orme, and had to return hurriedly along the whole length of the Parade about nine o'clock. And through every ground-floor window of every house he saw a long table full of people eating and drinking the same kinds of food. In

Llandudno fifty thousand souls desired always to perform the same act at the same time; they wanted to be distracted and they would do anything for the sake of distraction, and would pay for the privilege. And they would all pay at once. This great thought was more majestic to him than the sea or the Great Orme, or the Little Orme . . .

. . . He simply could not stir out of the house without spending money, and often in ways quite unforeseen. Pier, minstrels, Punch and Judy, bathing, buns, ices, canes, fruit, chairs, row-boats, concerts, toffee, photographs, char-a-bancs: any of these expenditures was likely to happen whenever they went forth for a simple stroll. One might think that strolls were gratis, that the air was free! Error! If he had had the courage he would have left his purse in the house as Ruth invariably did. But men are moral cowards.

He had calculated thus: Return fare, four shillings a week. Agreed terms at boarding-house, twenty-five shillings a week. Total expenses per week, twenty-nine shillings – say thirty!

On the first day he spent fourteen shillings on nothing whatever – which was at the rate of five pounds a week of supplementary estimates! On the second day he spent nineteen shillings on nothing whatever.

On the Monday morning he was up early and off to Bursley to collect rents and manage estates. He had spent nearly five pounds beyond his expectations. Indeed, if by chance he had not gone to Llandudno with a portion of the previous week's rents in his pockets, he would have been in what the Five Towns call a fix.

On the Tuesday evening he returned to Llandudno, and, despite the general trend of his thoughts, it once more occurred that his pockets were loaded with a portion of the week's rents. He did not know precisely what was going to happen, but he knew that something was going to happen; for the sufficient reason that his career could not continue unless something did happen.

What immediately happened was a storm at sea. He heard it mentioned at Rhyl, and he saw, in the deep night, the foam of breakers at Prestatyn. And when the train reached Llandudno, those two girls in ulsters and caps greeted him with wondrous tales of the storm at sea, and of wrecks, and of lifeboats. And they were so jolly, and so welcoming, so plainly glad to see their cavalier again, that Denry instantly discovered himself to be in the highest spirits. He put away the dark and brooding thoughts which had disfigured his journey, and became the gay Denry of his own dreams. The very wind intoxicated him. There was no rain.

It was half-past nine, and half Llandudno was afoot on the Parade and discussing the storm – a storm unparalleled, it seemed, in the month of August. At any rate, people who had visited Llandudno yearly for twenty-five years declared that never had they witnessed such a storm. The new lifeboat had gone forth, amid cheers, about six o'clock to a schooner in distress near Rhos, and at eight o'clock a second lifeboat (an old one which the new one had replaced and which had been bought for a floating warehouse by an aged fisherman) had departed to the rescue of a Norwegian barque, *the Hjalmar*; round the bend of the Little Orme.

'Let's go on the pier,' said Denry. 'It will be splendid.'

He was not an hour in the town, and yet was already hanging expense!

'They've closed the pier,' the girls told him.

But when in the course of their meanderings among the excited crowd under the gas-lamps they arrived at the pier-gates, Denry perceived figures on the pier.

'They're sailors and things, and the Mayor,' the girls explained.

'Pooh!' said Denny, fired.

He approached the turnstile and handed a card to the

43

official. It was the card of an advertisement agent of the *Staffordshire Signal*, who had called at Brougham Street in Denry's absence about the renewal of Denry's advertisement.

'Press,' said Denry to the guardian at the turnstile, and went through with the ease of a bird on the wing.

'Come along,' he cried to the girls.

The guardian seemed to hesitate.

'These ladies are with me,' he said.

The guardian yielded.

It was a triumph for Denry. He could read his triumph in the eyes of his companions. When she looked at him like that, Ruth was assuredly marvellous among women, and any ideas derogatory to her marvellousness which he might have had at Bursley and in the train were false ideas.

At the head of the pier beyond the pavilion, there were gathered together some fifty people, and the tale ran that the second lifeboat had successfully accomplished its mission and was approaching the pier.

'I shall write an account of this for the *Signal*,' said Denry, whose thoughts were excusably on the Press.

'Oh, do!' exclaimed Nellie.

'They have the *Signal* at all the newspaper shops here,' said Ruth. Then they seemed to be merged in the storm. The pier shook and trembled under the shock of the waves, and occasionally, though the tide was very low, a sprinkle of water flew up and caught their faces. The eyes could see nothing save the passing glitter of the foam on the crest of a breaker. It was the most thrilling situation that any of them had ever been in.

And at last came word from the mouths of men who could apparently see as well in the dark as in daylight, that the second lifeboat was close to the pier. And then everybody momentarily saw it – a ghostly thing that heaved up pale out of the murk for an instant, and was lost again.

And the little crowd cheered.

The next moment a Bengal light illuminated the pier, and the lifeboat was silhouetted with strange effectiveness against the storm. And someone flung a rope, and then another rope arrived out of the sea, and fell on Denry's shoulder.

'Haul on there!' yelled a hoarse voice. The Bengal light expired.

Denry hauled with a will. The occasion was unique. And those few seconds were worth to him the whole of Denry's precious life – yes, not excluding the seconds in which he had kissed Ruth and the minutes in which he had danced with the Countess of Chell. Then two men with beards took the rope from his hands. The air was now alive with shoutings. Finally there was a rush of men down the iron stairway to the lower part of the pier, ten feet nearer the water.

'You stay here, you two!' Denry ordered.

'But, Denry—'

'Stay here, I tell you!' All the male in him was aroused. He was off, after the rush of men. 'Half a jiffy,' he said, coming back. 'Just take charge of this, will you?' And he poured into their hands about twelve shillings' worth of copper, small change of rents, from his hip-pocket. 'If anything happened, that might sink me,' he said, and vanished.

It was very characteristic of him, that effusion of calm sagacity in a supreme emergency

The next morning at 5.20 the youthful sun was shining on the choppy water of the Irish Sea, just off the Little Orme, to the west of Llandudno Bay. Oscillating on the uneasy waves was Denry's lifeboat, manned by the nodding bearded head, three ordinary British longshoremen, a Norwegian who could speak English of two syllables, and two other Norwegians who by a strange neglect of

45

education could speak nothing but Norwegian.

Close under the headland, near a morsel of beach lay the remains of the *Hjalmar* in an attitude of repose. It was as if the *Hjalmar*, after a long struggle, had lain down like a cab-horse and said to the tempest:

'Do what you like now!'

'Yes,' the venerable head was piping. 'Us can come out comfortable in twenty minutes, unless the tide be setting east strong. And, as for getting back, it'll be the same, other way round, if ye understand me.

There could be no question that Simeon had come out comfortable. But he was the coxswain. The rowers seemed to be perspiringly aware that the boat was vast and beamy.

'Shall we row up to it?' Simeon inquired, pointing to the wreck. Then a pale face appeared above the gunwale, and an expiring, imploring voice said: 'No. We'll go back.' Whereupon the pale face vanished again.

Denry had never before been outside the bay. In the navigation of pantechnicons on the squall-swept basins of canals he might have been a great master, but he was unfitted for the open sea. At that moment he would have been almost ready to give the lifeboat and all that he owned for the privilege of returning to land by train. The inward journey was so long that Denry lost hope of ever touching his native island again. And then there was a bump. And he disembarked, with hope burning up again cheerfully in his bosom. And it was a quarter to six . . .

. . . At ten o'clock two Norwegian sailors, who could only smile in answer to the questions which assailed them, were distributing the following handbill on the Parade:

WRECK OF THE *HJALMAR*
HEROISM AT LLANDUDNO

Every hour, at 11, 12, 1, 2, 3, 4, 5, and 6 o'clock. THE
IDENTICAL (guaranteed) LIFEBOAT which rescued the
crew of the
HJALMAR
will leave the beach for the scene of the wreck. Manned by
Simeon Edwards, the oldest boatman in LLANDUDNO, and
by members of the rescued crew, genuine Norwegians
(guaranteed)
SIMEON EDWARDS, *Coxswain*
Return Fare, with use of Cork Belt and Lifelines
if desired, 2s. 6d.
A UNIQUE OPPORTUNITY
A UNIQUE EXPERIENCE
P.S. – The bravery of the lifeboatmen has been the theme of
the Press throughout the Principality and neighbouring
counties.

E.D. MACHIN

At eleven o'clock there was an eager crowd down on the
beach where, with some planks and a piece of rock, Simeon
had arranged an embarkation pier for the lifeboat. One man,
in over-ails, stood up to his knees in the water and escorted
passengers up the planks, while Simeon's confidence-
generating beard received them into the broad waist of the
boat. The rowers wore sou'-westers and were secured to the
craft by life-lines, and these conveniences were also offered,
with lifebelts, to the intrepid excursionists. A paper was
pinned in the stern: 'Licensed to carry Fourteen.' (Denry had
just paid the fee.) But quite forty people were anxious to
make the first voyage.

'No more,' shrilled Simeon, solemnly. And the wader
scrambled in and the boat slid away.

'Fares, please!' shrilled Simeon.

He collected one pound fifteen, and slowly buttoned it up in the right-hand pocket of his blue trousers.

Arnold Bennett (1867-1931): The Card

A Walk Around Conwy

We first walked round the exterior of the wall, at the base of which are hovels, with dirty children playing about them, and pigs rambling along, and squalid women visible in the doorways; but all these things melt into the picturesqueness of the scene, and do not harm it. The whole town of Conway is built in what was once the castle yard, and the whole circuit of the wall is still standing in a delightful state of decay. At the angles, and at regular intervals, there are round towers, having half their circle on the outside of the walls, and half within. Most of these towers have a great crack pervading them irregularly from top to bottom; the ivy hangs upon them, – the weeds grow on the tops. Gateways, three or four of them, open through the walls, and streets proceed from them into the town. At some points, very old cottages or small houses are close against the sides, and, old as they are, they must have been built after the whole structure was a ruin. in one place I saw the sign of an ale-house painted on the grey stones of one of the old round towers. As we entered one of the gates, after making the entire circuit, we saw an omnibus coming down the street towards us, with its horn sounding. Llandudno was its-place of destination; and, knowing no more about it than that it was four miles off, we took our seats.

Nathaniel Hawthorne (1804-1864): The English Notebooks

Incident at Conwy

During the Wars of the Roses a Lancastrian officer at Tal-y-Sarnau was shot by a marksman from the battlements of Conwy Castle. At this point the river is at least half a mile wide. The feat was recorded by several chroniclers.

1 Llewelyn of Nannau

Oh man, you are foolish to wear that surcoat.
The blue and the gold outrage the dull afternoon.
You are a heraldic flicker among the leaves,
tempting my pride.
I have not killed men in the stench and fury
of battle only, that I would baulk at this.
I am an archer. I send death winging,
sudden, and cold, over parapet and fosse;
the lightning that strikes nowhere twice.
I am too far away to see your pain;
the blood that will sully your bright coat.
Too far to hear the shriek from your lady's arbour.
Nor will imagination spoil my aim.
The taut string creaks against my fingers,
brushes my cheek softly, as I draw back.
My eye is steady down the shaven shaft.
You are a roebuck, a proud stag, a target.
Your words do not goad me, I cannot hear what you say.
Your death will be skillfully given, and without rancour,
At least I am not too far from you for that.

2 Rhys ap Gruffudd Goch

The river is wide, and the leaves cover us;
we are safe enough – but they are certainly ready.
Each tower and arrowslit is crowded with faces.
and notice the fool on the battlements with his bow.
This castle will drink an oblation of blood
before we break its stone teeth.

That archer has seen me; he lifts his bow.
Well, the river will not bleed from his arrow.
Doubtless he would kill me if he could
land boast about it over the spilled wine;
a distant, stout, nameless man,
who would never have seen my face.

Then he would thresh about in the straw at night,
seek solace from priests, drink away memory.
But the line would have been thrown between us,
he bright gift passed, that he could not take back.
Look, he draws. *If* he should strike me down
I will never be so far from him again.

                                        Catherine Fisher

Change of Weather at Conwy

Chimney-smoke curling from slate roofs
Then blowing out seaward like a squall.
Sky lightening momentarily – magnolia-petalled,
Shifting a sifting of cloud against castle parapets
(A feather-light caress as flesh warms on flesh)
And pouring a prism of yellow
Laser-angled at Deganwy.
(Caught in the glow and melting within sunlit rooms.)

Gulls standing sentinel, spanning
Turret, quay and quiff of a wave,
(From stronghold to height in rhythm with the sea)
Their cries echoing history through dank castle walls
Of battles fought in fervour – now extinguished.
(Enmeshed, entangled, abandoned in sheer exhaustion
Like nets along the quay.)

Frances Sackett

Llys Helig

Out in the bay, underneath the sea, lie the remains of Llys
Helig, once a castle and a town surrounded by meadows
and orchards and fields of grain. An idyllic spot, except that,
as so often happens, its ruler was a truly nasty piece of
work, who spread fear and corruption throughout the land.
He had respect neither for God nor man and never drew a
sober breath. He gave the sort of parties that last all week,
inciting his guests to behave worse and worse until they lay
around in heaps, exhausted, comatose and blind with liquor.

He was warned several times by the more responsible members of the community that this behaviour could lead to no good. The harpist in particular was loud in his protests and denunciations (for some reason harpists always were), but the ruler took no notice, apart from killing a few people who he considered had gone too far and were too impudent and irritating to live. His subjects cowered in their huts, bowed down with apprehension, fearing both the wrath of their overlord and the dreadful consequences that his Cities-of-the-Plain lifestyle would bring upon them all.

Unearthly voices were heard in the night, crying vengeance, and no one slept easy in his bed, nor was able, in the morning, to take untroubled delight in the loveliness of the fertile fields and groves. One evening during the course of an orgy, spectacular even by his standards, the sky grew prematurely dark.

'Looks like rain,' said Helig, staring with unfocused eyes at the deepening shadows. 'Have another drink.'

His five wolfhounds, three dogs and two bitches, who had been lying sucking the marrow out of some venison bones, got up from the floor, all strewn as it was with decaying rushes and the remains of old feasts, and began to pace uneasily up and down, sniffing the wind and whimpering.

'Lie down, you dogs,' roared their master. 'Heel.'

But they had leapt up the steps of the great chamber and were streaking towards the hills, the hair on the back of their necks sticking up straight. The ruler rallied a moment from his stupor to promise himself he would flay them alive when they came back, and called for another barrel of mead.

'Storm at sea,' he muttered, as the skies grew darker and the shadows crept closer.

The old manservant doddered, rush light in hand, down through the blackness to where the drink was kept. He was up again in no time, shaking with shock, and his feet wet.

'Sire, Sire,' he gasped, 'the fishes are swimming in the cellars.'

'Don't be such a bloody fool,' said Helig, 'or I'll have your ears cut off.'

Trembling, the old man contrived to drag a barrel into the banqueting hall. Already the mead tasted of salt, but Helig was too far gone to notice.

'Aargh,' said the old man after a while, 'Sire, the fishes are swimming about your feet.'

'If you don't shut up,' roared Helig, 'I'll have your eyes put out.'

He clambered on to a low dais where the harpist had been wont to sit, strumming his warnings and singing his lays. He quaffed his mead and gazed, half-seeing, at his unconscious guests lying all around. They did look a bit damp and the fire had gone out.

'Superstitious nonsense,' grumbled Helig to himself, trying to draw his feet up out of the sea.

'Sire, Sire,' screamed the old manservant, who had prudently left the castle, uttering his third warning, 'the fishes are swimming through the windows.'

'If you say that once more,' whispered Helig, 'I'll cut off your – glug, glug, glug . . . '

The sober and industrious peasants had gathered up whatever they could carry and had fled, led by the harpist and the old manservant, away from the waves which had first crept and then tumbled all over their lands, and crouched, wringing their hands and blind with weeping, at a place called Trwyn y Wylfa – The Point of Wailing – high on the hill.

I have bad tea at the farmhouse there too. Sometimes at iow tide you can see the gaunt remains of Helig's castle – or perhaps it's only a natural rock formation. Who knows? The past is inaccessible to us and all we have is the stories the old men tell. Or perhaps it is all true and the accursed Helig is responsible still for the sense of death that hangs over that stretch of road. If his unquiet spirit still walks beneath the waves out there I wonder what it will make of the four-lane highway – or, as it is called, the Expressway. I suppose one could take the view that it will serve him right.

Alice Thomas Ellis: A Welsh Childhood (1990)

Above Penmaenmawr

The upland farmers have all gone;
the lane they laid twists without purpose,
visiting broken gates and overgrown
gardens, to end in clumps of gorse.

Their unroofed houses and fallen barns,
rich in nettles, lie dead in hiding
from the wind that howls off Talyfan's
saw-tooth ridge; their walls divide

bracken from bracken; their little church
of bare rock has outlasted use:
hikers' signatures in the porch,
Keys obtainable at the Guesthouse'.

Yet, not to sentimentalize,
their faces turned from drudgery
when the chance showed itself. There is
hardly a sign of the husbandry

of even the last to leave – so slight
was their acceptance by the land.
They left for the seaside towns, to get
easier jobs, and cash in hand.

Five miles of uplands, and beyond –
a thousand feet below – the coast,
its bright lights twinkling; freezing wind
dragging the cloud down like a frost

from Talyfan. Alone upon
these darkening, silent heights, my fears
stay stubbornly with the farmers, gone
after six hundred thankless years.

Tony Connor

© Poet

This Great Mountain Promontory

I pursued the road following the sweep of the coast towards Penmaen Mawr, whose rocky, precipitous base, running out in a bluff promontory, projects into the waves. In the course of the afternoon, while pausing on an eminence to contemplate the features of the landscape, I beheld at a distance a vast rainbow, stretching its purple-tinged radius from shore to shore. It was a glorious spectacle. The contrast of the many-coloured bow with the dark waters, the sparkling clearness of the sky above, the brightness of the sunshine resting on the surrounding hills, and the various features of the nearer scenery formed altogether so magnificent a scene, that even the traveller in the grander regions of the Valais or Savoy can seldom witness anything more sublime.

It was towards nightfall when I approached that part of my journey where the road, hewn out of the solid rock, was like a terrace midway along the face of the mountain, many hundred feet above the sea, which breaks in thunder below. The evening was mild and beautiful. Clouds, slightly charged with lightning, hung over sea and land; and from time to time bright flashes, unaccompanied by thunder, kindled the firmament, –showing momentarily the form of the clouds, and gleaming over the face of the ocean. Occasionally the eye caught, by this transient light, glimpses of the black, beetling rocks overhanging the road, communicating to them a gloomy grandeur of character which I should in vain endeavour to describe. Formerly, before the road had been widened, and defended by a parapet, this passage of Penmaen Mawr was full of danger. But, though terrific, it is now perfectly safe; unless we contemplate the possibility of the rain or frost detaching, as it sometimes does, vast rocky fragments of the superincumbent mountain, and hurling them headlong upon the helpless traveller. Ideas of such catastrophes naturally enough present themselves, in such situations, to the mind; it was therefore not without pleasure that I found myself beyond the possibility of danger.

Correctly speaking, this great mountain promontory has two divisions, – one of which is called Penmaen Mawr, the other Penmaen Bach, – the latter lying the nearest to Conwy; but the whole is generally known to the tourist by the former name. Less than a century ago, a narrow zigzag path, along the side of the rock, was the only convenience for travellers.

At that time there was an inn at each end of the pass, and the witty Dean Swift is said to have composed the following couplets, which greeted the admiring traveller on the sign-posts as he entered and debouched from it:

'Before you venture here to pass,
Take a good refreshing glass.'

'Now you're over take another,
Your drooping spirits to recover.'

It was from the many accidents which occurred that the Legislature was induced, in 1772, to assist in carrying out the plan projected by Mr John Sylvester, and in forming the present grand terrace, which has more recently been further enlarged and improved under the direction of Mr Telford. It is well guarded on the sea side, and many of the overhanging fragments of rock have been blasted.

Thomas Roscoe (1753-1831):
Wanderings and Excursions in North Wales

Bangor Pier

(For Luned)

Do you remember the heron
We saw that morning
Poised on the rocks; the thrush bearing
A snail shell, like a death's head warning?

The long strolls on the broken pier
And the wind spying
About our legs with gusty leer,
Smelling of salt; the sea-weed drying

On the rusty ladders and bars;
Tea tuppence cheaper,
But no stronger. There went the cars
On Beaumaris road; the pier keeper,

Like a revolutionary,
Was always knitting,
And we, never in a hurry
For all our work, were always sitting,

Talking, there in the old, cold hut,
And getting nowhere,
Like the boat we watched, that would cut
Back from the steps, into the shattered air.

Sally Roberts Jones

Slate Quay: Felinheli

1

This will go too, this curve of shore
Which, bending the tangled Straits,
Looks over at fields that bulge smoothly
Under the folded church of Llanfairisgaer.

Today a brown clout of mist rushes
Over the grey, brawling waters.
The trees bow in anticipation
Curled by the wind's clinical hands
For the sudden drilling rape of rain
On their pale-bellied leaves.

Here, in this village which is asleep
And has not awoken for hundred of years,
On its blue and grey quayside
Swept of slate piles and inhabited
Now by tatty dogs, lone walkers
The strident gulls and suave
Motor-cruisers, the lives of men
Sing in moist air and the spirit
Of human life wanders, inconsolable,
Pitting a faded emphasis against the end.

2

The small dog which ran, paused, poised
Pissed on a bollard then tracked on swiftly
Has it all his own way.
The bridge waits for the axe

The locks leak and spurt
The arrogant yachts bump the wall
And look as if it were not there.
An old woman calls the dog which, deaf,
Maps out again its world of odours.

Two times are here but one will conquer
As the sleepwalking people
Twitch obediently to their till's song.

Peter Gruffydd: 'The Shimmering Seed'

A Bay in Anglesey

The sleepy sound of a tea-time tide
Slaps at the rocks the sun has dried,

Too lazy, almost, to sink and lift
Round low peninsulas pink with thrift.

The water, enlarging shells and sand,
Grows greener emerald out from land

And brown over shadowy shelves below
The waving forests of seaweed show.

Here at my feet in the short cliff grass
Are shells, dried bladderwrack, broken glass,

Pale blue squills and yellow rock roses.
The next low ridge that we climb discloses

One more field for the sheep to graze
While, scarcely seen on this hottest of days,

Far to the eastward, over there,
Snowdon rises in pearl-grey air.

Multiple lark-song, whispering bents,
The thymy, turfy and salty scents

And filling in, brimming in, sparkling and free
The sweet susurration of incoming sea.

John Betjeman (1906-1984):
'Collected Poems'

Trippers to Aberffraw

for Ray and Els

The village awkwardly pretends not to know
What violence was done here, or what craft
Intricate as Kells, was etched into the blood.

Falcon lord . . . head like a thrusting wolf . . .
White-as-millrace face of a girl

Litigations brilliant in verses
Of a grey court on the rocks hung over foam
Where London ambassadors heard all night
The cold Brythonic of curlews; or a young lad
Watched Sir Cormorant periscope for fishes –

The village awkwardly ignores it. Cottages
Of an undressed and barbarous stone, bestrode
By yellow Nonconformity like a slag tip

Where all the people seem somehow defective –
Lack leg or nose, or lisp, or quietly
Wander off, six months in the year, and no one knows.

The fourteenth-century Anglican church
Confides to itself a delegated past.

*   *   *

Geology forgets. The dunes grow big by night.
Curlews are crying from the salt profit
Of many moons. Sand's no legend-teller.
But the brilliant antiquity of the gold sun
Has summoned from this blown-about earth
A thousand flowers – tabby-faced pansies, bee
Orchis, succulents. Moonworts spike in the slack.
Though the light's a deal more ancient even than here,
Nothing – not even the sun – is as old as now.

*   *   *

You're off to Aberffraw? Curlews like Welsh bards
Will worry that such as you
Have come unmourningly
Glib as thieves' torches
Into their brittle Egypt of rock graves.

You reach the gold antiquity itself
Who ride your humping scooter to the sand
And lay out four slim legs for the sun to sign

And an idle toehold take of a tuft of grass,
Trickle and trickle fine fingerfuls of sand

Till the generous day leads home.

* * *

A red sky, boats like dried skulls, aground
    In scattered grey handfuls;
   Vociferously seagulls
   Cluster, hover round their hulls.

This village has come, somehow, all our glib
    Lies to disallow,
   Not free to be Aberffraw
   Names our sickness to us now.

* * *

I cannot face the eyes of here
Nor see along the sight of now.
I cannot night and day both focus,
Cold curlew cry and ramshackle town.

Insidiously the Princes wait
In grey-backed clusters calling of war.
Meanwhile your fingers in the idle sand
Trickle through peace, pain no more

Tony Conran: 'The Shape of my Country'

Waiting to Sail

24 September, 1727: 'I dined with an old Innkeeper, Mrs Welch, about 3, on a Loin of Mutton very good, but the worst ale in the world, and no wine, for the day before I came here a vast number went to Ireland after having drunk all the wine.' On the following day: 'The Captain talks of sailing at 12, The talk goes off, the wind is fair, but he says it is too fierce; I believe he wants more company,' The 26th: 'The weather is fiercer and wilder than yesterday, yet the Captain now dreams of sailing . . . I should be glad to talk with Farmers and Shopkeepers but none of them speak English. A Dog is better company than the Vicar, for I remember him of old . . . The Master of the packet-boat, one Jones, hath not treated me with the least civility, although Watt gave him my name. In short I come from being used like an Emperor to be used worse than a Dog at Holyhead. Yet my hat is worn to pieces by answering the civilities of the poor inhabitants as they pass by.' The 28th: 'Tis allowed that we learn patience by suffering. I have not spirit enough left me to fret . . . Well it is now three in the afternoon. I have dined and revisited the Master; the wind and tide serve, and I am just taking boat to go to the ship.' The 29th, Friday: 'You will now know something of what it is to be at sea. We had not been half an hour in the ship till a fierce wind rose directly against us; we tried a good while, but the storm still continued, so we turned back and it was 8 at night, dark and raining, before the ship got back at anchor. The other passengers went back in a boat to Holyhead, but to prevent accidents and broken shins I lay all night on board and came back this morning at 8. Am now in my chamber, where I must stay and get a fresh stock of patience.'

Jonathan Swift (1667-1745): Holyhead Journal

On Carmel Head

I want to tell you of three bays, and a walk that I made between them. The bays are all in the vicinity of Carmel Head, north-westerlymost point of Anglesey. It has about it an indefinable atmosphere – the west of mood as well as of place – that overwhelms you in regions as removed as Iona or Achill, Pen Llyn or Penwith. The first bay is Hen Borth, and it's typical of the small coves battered into this rough coastline. Great flat pebbles, browny-grey and heaped high as loaves in a Moroccan market, line the shore. Above, the cultivated land sweeps down almost to the cliff-tops. A dry, husky wind croons and trembles continually off the sea and through the fields of barley. Kestrels fly out of rabbit-holes and drift, red-brown shadows, over the rocks; coveys of partridge scatter at your approach, rabbits bolt and a peregrine's flight carves a scar across distance.

As you near Carmel Head itself, two beacons, white-painted to seaward, align themselves with that on the offshore rock of West Mouse to aid navigation through this difficult seaway. The light on The Skerries, which has shone since 1717, blinks out its two-second, ten-second rhythm. An old coppermine chimney lists crazily towards the ruined building beyond. You drop down green slopes studded in summer with sweet, round, nut-flavoured mushrooms that you can peel and eat raw, to the second bay, Porth yr Hwch.

There is a story located here, and it is one of the strangest I know. This coastline at the beginning of the eighteenth century was notorious for the smuggling activity that took place along it. On a stormy day one of these discreet outlaws was on the cliff-top above Porth yr Hwch, looking out for a cargo of contraband. He saw a raft drifting into the cove with two figures on it, half-drowned, and scrambled down to them. They were children, spoke no English. He took them to the farm of Maes by the church at Llanfair-yng-

Nghornwy. One of them died. The other was adopted, given the name of Evan, and showed remarkable skill in the setting of bones, at first of animals, but as his reputation grew, in time of people too. He, and his son and grandson in their turn, became famous throughout North Wales as *meddygon esgyrn* – bonesetters. His great-grandson was the pioneer orthopaedic surgeon Hugh Owen Thomas, his great-great grandson Sir Robert Jones, who founded the orthopaedic hospital at Gobowen, and whose skill and invention saved the limbs of thousands of soldiers in the Great War. I find it so strange to think a lineage that did so much to alleviate human suffering should by chance have been cast ashore here, on this wild headland. But not so strange as I find the suffering humanity is still willing to impose here on mute creation.

Jim Perrin: Spirits of Place (1997)

In Memory of James and Frances Williams

(Founders of the first lifeboat in Ynys Môn)

The sea's tumbling escalator
beside them, they had a nickname

for the operator of it,
Davy Jones – an effort to domesticate

a monster. They peered
into his locker and saw bodies

like weeds dancing the dance
of the long dead. They leaned

from the bucking row-boat
to extend a hand to the living,

and so an association was formed
that was to rescue its thousands.

What can a stone say?
The only creases
on its forehead are
the lines of blurred print

the weather is erasing.
'In memory of' — the churchyards
are far off, yet this
is the headstone over

a myriad graves. To what
end this expenditure
of good granite? The sea
smiles and is never

to be trusted. Steam
has drawn the teeth
of the snags and skerries,
and the light drops only

a stone tear for the broken
masts and the torn sails.
But the gulls remember
the crews' wailing, and far

from the shore, as though
hands were lifted, the waving
goes on from casualties
surfacing for the last time.

Light steers to safety.
It steered in warped
hands vessels on the rocks.
Yet courage is that
which the good and evil
possess in common.
It was indiscriminate here;
the wreckers' relations
manned the first of
the life-boats. Grips had to be
prised from intolerable
oar-handles; and the Church
was there, putting prayer
into action, wringing from heretical
rollers a reluctant Amen.

We are mastering the planet.
The tide's pendulum is that
of a stopped clock where
hazardry is concerned. High

over precipitous breakers
the 'planes fly, ironing them
smooth. The brave answer
of the coxwain: 'We need

not come back, but we have
to go out' has shrunk
to a whisper. Put your ear
to this stone, so you may hear it still.

R.S. Thomas (1913-2000)

A Great Broken Ship

. . . the moment nothing was so calmly and monotonously real under the sunlight as the gentle rising and falling of the water with its freight, the regular turning of the windlass aboard the Lighter, and the slight obstruction so very near my feet.

O reader, haply turning this page by the fireside at Home, and hearing the night wind rumble in the chimney, that slight obstruction was the uppermost fragment of the Wreck of the *Royal Charter*, Australian trader and passenger ship, homeward bound, that struck here on the terrible morning of the twenty-sixth of this October, broke into three parts, went down with her treasure of at least five hundred human lives, and has never stirred since!

From which point, or from which, she drove ashore, stem foremost; on which side, or on which, she passed the little Island in the bay, for ages henceforth to be aground certain yards outside her; these are rendered bootless questions by the darkness of that night and the darkness of death. Here she went down.

Even as I stood on the beach with the words 'Here she went down!' in my ears, a diver in his grotesque dress, dipped heavily over the side of the boat alongside the Lighter, and dropped to the bottom.

Only two short months had gone, since a man, living on the nearest hill-top overlooking the sea, being blown out of bed at about daybreak by the wind that had begun to strip his roof off, and getting upon a ladder with his nearest neighbour to construct some temporary device for keeping his house over his head, saw from the ladder's elevation as he looked down by chance towards the shore, some dark troubled object close in with the land. And he and the other, descending to the beach, and finding the sea mercilessly beating over a great broken ship, had clambered up the stony ways, like staircases without stairs, on which the wild village hangs in little clusters, as fruit hangs on boughs, and had given the alarm. And so, over the hill-slopes, and past the waterfall, and down the gullies where the land drains off into the ocean, the scattered quarrymen and fisher-men inhabiting that part of Wales had come running to the dismal sight – their clergyman among them. And as they stood in the leaden morning, stricken with pity, leaning hard against the wind, their breath and vision often failing as the sleet and spray rushed at them from the ever forming and dissolving mountains of sea, and as the wool which was a part of the vessel's cargo blew in with the salt foam and remained upon the land when the foam melted, they saw the ship's life-boat put off from one of the heaps of wreck; and first, there were three men in her, and in a moment she capsized, and there were but two; and again, she was struck by a vast mass of water, and there was but one; and again, she was thrown bottom upward, and that one, with his arm struck through the broken planks and waving as if for the help that could never reach him, went down into the deep.

It was the clergyman himself from whom I heard this, while I stood on the shore, looking in his kind wholesome face as it turned to the spot where the boat had been. The divers were down then, and busy. They were 'lifting' to-day the gold found yesterday – some five-and-twenty thousand pounds. Of three hundred and fifty thousand pounds' worth of gold, three hundred thousands pounds' worth, in round numbers, was at that time recovered. The great bulk of the remainder was surely and steadily coming up. Some loss of sovereigns there would be, of course; indeed, at first sovereigns had drifted in with the sand, and been scattered far and wide over the beach, like sea-shells.

He had the church keys in his hand, and opened the churchyard gate, and opened the church door; and we went in.

It is a little church of great antiquity; there is reason to believe that some church has occupied the spot, these thousand years or more. The pulpit was gone, and other things usually belonging to the church were gone, owing to its living congregation having deserted it for the neighbouring school-room, and yielded it up to the dead. The very Commandments had been shouldered out of their places, in the bringing in of the dead; the black wooden tables on which they were painted, were askew, and on the stone pavement below them, and on the stone pavement all over the church, were the marks and stains where the drowned had been laid down. The eye, with little or no aid from the imagination, could yet see how the bodies had been turned, and where the head had been and where the feet. Some faded traces of the wreck of the Australian ship may be discernible on the stone pavement of this little church, hundreds of years hence, when the digging for gold in Australia shall have long and long ceased out of the land.

Charles Dickens (1812-1870): The Uncommercial Traveller

Wreck of the Royal Charter

(The vicar of Penrhos Lligwy is said to have died as a result of strain and overwork after the wreck)

He gave, to begin with, his duty.
The appropriate words
Written out in a hundred letters:
'Dear madam . . . he did not suffer,'
'Your daughter is with God,'
'The loss was rapid;
They cannot have felt much pain.'

What else could he write?
That the wreck had taken hours?
That slowly they saw their hopes
Destroyed, and knew
All of the horror of dying?
That Tom from the shop
Had drowned while his father watched
Ten yards away?

He gave, to begin with, his duty,
Assuming command;
Wrote letters, saw relatives,
Presided at funerals; tried
Preserving the souls of his flock
From a hundred sins,
And the wrath of an ignorant world.

In the end he was giving too much:
He died of the wreck,
Drowned in the wash of their deaths,
In the deeps of their fear,
Giving comfort to others,
Who, having no knowledge of death,
Had no need of the comfort he gave.

Sally Roberts Jones

Crossing a Shore

It was, that day,
September the second.
And here we were, as a family,
Deciding to go to the sea.

It was, that day,
Sunny though a bit windy.
Over the great, empty shore
The wind would shake
The brightnesses of the sun,
Would whistle its yellow across the sand
And sparkle the water on the tide's far ebb.

And here we were, starting to do the things
That people do on beaches
Shovel sand;
Put the baby to sit in the salty
Marvel of it; build castles; kick a ball.
The boys even went bathing
As though they'd a duty to.

But it was, that day,
Too cold to stay long in the water.
I just stood watching.

They came glistening out of the sea, their teeth
Chattering, laughing and splashing,
And here they were then, running in front of me
Across the long beach
To their mam, to their sister,
To shelter and towels.

I just followed at a distance.
But as I crossed the beach, about halfway,
It struck me with a shock
That this happens only once.

What I was doing would never, never come back.
Even the moment just gone
Is gripped within eternity
Fast as the Iron Age.
That's what it means, our mortality.
And I felt a bit lost then
This thing won't ever happen again.

But I kept on walking
And before long I came back
To the family,
To the palaver of drying and changing,
To the sound of the present.
And what with digging the sand
And crunching through a tomato sandwich
And trying to calm the baby
That sense of loss went by.

I had, as it happened,
My birthday that day.
I was forty-one.

There's an old Russian proverb which says,
'Life is not crossing a field.'
Correct: it is crossing a shore.

Gwyn Thomas, translated by Tony Conran

Interlude at Traeth Bychan

It was the summer of *The Magus*.

He did what men do when they are young
beside the sea – lazed or swam,
anointed himself with oil,
watched children digging, quarrelling,
building castles with tacky sand
which they or the sea would soon flatten.
Timeless tides came and went.

He opened the book on a second island
where a labyrinth swallowed him.
There was a magician with a revolver,
there was a girl, slim and elusive.
He floated in another sea,
was tanned by another sun.
He read: *Greece is like a mirror.*

Flank to flank, in a black bikini,
she lay sleeping or half-asleep.
Freckles scattered across her skin.
Her dark hair dropped to her shoulders,
letting the sunlight lacquer it.
In the lenses of her sunglasses,
his eyes looked back at him.

At night they took the cliff path
to the village with one pub. The beer
disgusted them. They returned beneath
a peach-slice of moon, generous stars.
Catching at their clothing, brambles
had to be unhooked. And the sea? Always
hushing itself, it never seemed to sleep –

unlike the two of them in the caravan
in the quarry out of sight of the bay,
tired by love-making and the inertia of the day.
It was a story without a plot, just
a simple narrative. It directed him to wake
to a sunny island's tumbled rocks,
blue water, a girl with brown hair

and a book with unread pages

Richard Poole

Editor's note: John Fowles' novel *The Magus* was published
in the nineteen-sixties and has a Greek setting.

Daydreaming

I would like you to daydream with me, as the dawn's eyeball rolls feverishly in the night's black socket. I am a wrecker with a lantern, luring ships onto the shore, like the 18th century wreckers of Crigyll on the west coast of Anglesey. I thought wreckers were illiterate ruffians living in caves until I read about these Welsh mooncussers: on the contrary, they were upstanding members of the community – a farmer, a weaver, a tailor, a housewife, and children were among them; a chapel elder discovered some of his own congregation at it.

If you visit Beaumaris Courthouse you will learn about the famous case of 1741 when four of the robbers were arraigned before the island's chief justice, Thomas Martyn, who also happened to be a notorious lush. The wreckers' families disrupted the trial and Thomas Martyn made a drunken hash of things, so the men got away with it. But the wreckers had committed a particularly heinous crime, and they had a grim avenger on their trail. William Chilcott, captain of a sloop called the Charming Jenny, had been lured onto the rocks in a storm and had witnessed the wreckers murdering his wife by holding her head under water until she drowned. They broke a finger to remove her gold wedding ring and her body was stripped of valuables. Despite setbacks, Chilcott eventually got the men tried at Shrewsbury, and two were sentenced to death (although only one seems to have been hanged).

Lloyd Jones: Mr Vogel (2004)

The Thieves of Crigyll

'How fine to the good and honest
Is the light of candle and fire;
How fine to the brigands of the night
Is to be in darkened houses;
How fine to my ears is it to hear
Of the hanging of the Thieves of Crigyll.

It is a village without the fear of God,
Where evil lies in the hearts of men,
Bandits of the waves, vicious villains
Hiding their lanterns under their cloaks;
May God keep innocent travellers
From wrecking on the rocks of Crigyll.'

Lewis Morris (1701-1765): Translated from the Welsh

Welsh Incident

'But that was nothing to what things came out
From the sea-caves of Criccieth yonder.'
'What were they? Mermaids? dragons? ghosts?'
'Nothing at all of any things like that.'
'What were they, then?'

　　　　　　　　　　　　'All sorts of queer things,
Things never seen or heard or written about,
Very strange, un-Welsh, utterly peculiar
Things. Oh, solid enough they seemed to touch,
Had anyone dared it. Marvellous creation,
All various shapes and sizes, and no sizes,
All new, each perfectly unlike his neighbour,

Though all came moving slowly out together.'
'Describe just one of them.

                                                'I am unable.'

'What were their colours?'

                                'Mostly nameless colours,
Colours you'd like to see; but one was puce
Or perhaps more like crimson, but not purplish.
Some had no colour.'

                                'Tell me, had they legs?'
'Not a leg nor foot among them that I saw.'
'But did these things come out in any order?
What o'clock was it? What was the day of the week?
Who else was present? How was the weather?'
'I was coming to that, It was half-past three
On Easter Tuesday last. The sun was shining.
The Harlech Silver Band played *Marchog Iesu*
On thirty-seven shimmering instruments,
Collecting for Caernarvon's (Fever) Hospital Fund.
The populations of Pwllheli, Criccieth,
Portmadoc, Borth, Tremadoc, Penrhyndeudraeth
Were all assembled. Criccieth's mayor addressed them
First in good Welsh and then in fluent English,
Twisting his fingers in his chain of office,
Welcoming the things. They came out on the sand,
Not keeping time to the band, moving seaward
Silently at a snail's pace. But at last
The most odd, indescribable thing of all,
Which hardly one man there could see for wonder,
Did something recognizably a something.'
'Well, what?'

                        'It made a noise.'

                                        'A frightening noise?'
'No, no.

                'A musical noise? A noise of scuffling?'
'No, but a very loud, respectable noise—

Like groaning to oneself on Sunday morning
In Chapel, close before the second psalm.'
'What did the mayor do?'

'I was coming to that.'

Robert Graves (1895-1985)

Welsh Incident

*(In the early hours of September 3rd, 1997, a giant turtle was
found dead, on the shoreline at Criccieth)*

The Cambrian News reporter's car
blocks the lane down to the shore.

Someone plays the bagpipes
where the last field meets the sea.

But for the randomness of the tide
she'd still be gracing the waters
of a century as it drowned.

Armour-plated, run aground,
a creaturely grief mourns her end.

Two elderly, village paparazzi
circle the wreckage, take snaps
before the oceanographers descend.

Paul Henry: The Bread Thief

Young Fellow From Llŷn

Young fellow from Llŷn, who's the girl of your heart,
You who wander so late in the evening apart?
My sweetheart is young and she comes from the Sarn,
And neat is her cottage that's under the Garn.

And what does she look like, the girl of your heart,
You who wander so late in the evening apart?
Dark, dark is my darling and dark haired is she,
But white shines her body like foam on the sea.

And what is she wearing, the girl of your heart,
You who wander so late in the evening apart?
In a long gown of shining white satin she goes
And red in her bosom there blushes a rose.

Young fellow from Llŷn, is she angry and flown,
That you wander so late in the evening alone?
Oh, never my sweetheart showed anger or pride
Since the very first time that we walked side by side.

Young fellow from Llŷn, why do tears then start
To your eyes as you wander so late and apart?
From her cheek Death has withered the roses away
And white is the wear in the cottage of clay.

William Jones (1896-1961),
translated by Harri Webb

Abersoch

There was that headland, asleep on the sea,
The air full of thunder and the far air
Brittle with lightning; there was that girl
Riding her cycle, hair at half-mast,
And the men smoking, the dinghies at rest
On the calm tide. There were people going
About their business, while the storm grew
Louder and nearer and did not break.

Why do I remember these few things,
That were rumours of life, not life itself
That was being lived fiercely, where the storm raged?
Was it just that the girl smiled,
Though not at me, and the men smoking
Had the look of those who have come safely home?

R.S. Thomas (1913-2000)

Aberdaron

When I am old and honoured,
    With silver in my purse,
All criticism over,
    All men singing my praise,
I will purchase a lonely cottage
    With nothing facing its door
But the cliffs of Aberdaron
    And the wild waves on the shore.

When I am old and honoured,
    And my blood is running chill,
And watching the moon rising
    Stirs in my heart no thrill,
Hope will be mine thereafter
    In a cottage with its door
To the cliffs of Aberdaron
    And the wild waves on the shore.

When I am old and honoured
    Beyond all scorn and acclaim,
And my song goes by the rubric
    And gone is its passion's flame,
Hope will be mine thereafter
    In a cottage with its door
To the cliffs of Aberdaron
    And the wild waves on the shore.

For there I will discover
    In the stormy wind and its cry
Echoes of the old rebellion
    My soul knew in days gone by.
And I will sing with the old passion
    While gazing through the door
At the cliffs of Aberdaron
    And the wild waves on the shore.

Cynan (1895-1970),
translated by Joseph P. Clancy

Schoonermen

Great in this,
They made small ships do
Big things, leaping hurdles
Of the stiff sea, horse against horses
In the tide race.

What has Rio
To do with Pwllheli? Ask winds
Bitter for ever
With their black shag. Ask the quays
Stained with spittle.

Four days out

With bad cargo
Fever took the crew;
The mate and boatswain,
Peering in turn
Through the spray's window,
Brought her home. Memory aches
In the bones' rigging. If tales were tall,
Waves were taller.

From long years
In a salt school, caned by brine,
They came landward
With the eyes of boys,
The Welsh accent
Thick in their sails.

R.S. Thomas (1913-2000),

In Bardsey Sound

(Hilaire Belloc's 'The Cruise of the Nona' describes a journey by sea around part of the British coastline)

I looked at the Carnarvonshire coast there close at hand, the sinking lines of the mountains as they fell into the sea, and I discovered myself to be for the first time in my life entirely indifferent to my fate . . .

Anyhow, here I was in Bardsey Sound, with many deaths moving over the howling fury of the sea, and not one of them affecting me so much as a shadow passing over a field.

The end of that adventure was odd and unreasonable – as things will be at sea. It was perhaps because we had been buffeted and pushed into some edge of the conflict between wind and water where the tide runs slacker; or it was perhaps because the wind had risen still higher. But, at any rate, after three separate raids forward (in the second of which we were very nearly out of our peril and into smooth water), and as many set-backs (one of which got us into the worst violence we had yet suffered) the *Nona*, in a fourth attempt (it was her own, not ours – we could do nothing but keep her, as best we might, to her course), slipped out and reached an eddy beyond the tide. For a moment it was very difficult to keep her to it, she slewed round; but then again she got her head southerly, and we found ourselves running past the great Black Rock which stands there – the Carrig Dhu – and marks the smooth water beyond the edge of the tide.

We breathed again; and as I took her on through an easy sea, close under the land with not too much strain upon the helm (for the high shore now broke the gale), I was free to look over my right shoulder and watch, passing away behind us, further and further, the hell of white water and noise, through which we had barely come to safety.

Danger keeps men awake and makes them forget necessity, but with this relief, our fatigue came upon us. My friend and I had now been awake for some twenty-five or twenty-six hours, and it was time for sleep.

We got the poor *Nona* which had behaved so well, up into a lonely little bay where was an old abandoned mine working, but no other sign of man. The Welshman with us told it was good holding ground; we let go the anchor and stowed sail. I remember how I fell half asleep as I stretched the cover over the mainsail boom and yard and tied it down at the after end. The gale still blew, yet, as it seemed, more steadily and less fiercely. There was no danger of dragging. We were well under the lee of the land. I gave one look, under the violent but clear morning sky, to seaward before I went below; and there I saw how, at a certain distance from the land, in a long line, the white water began. It was like being in a lagoon, like being protected by a bank from the sea outside; but really it was only the effect of the lee of the land making a belt of smooth water along shore. Then we all lay down to sleep and slept till evening.

Hilaire Belloc (1870-1953): The Cruise of the Nona

Enlli

(for Ceri when she was ten)

We get to it through troughs and rainbows

falling and flying

rocked in an eggshell
over drowned mountain ranges.

The island swings towards us, slowly.

We slide in on an oiled keel.
Step ashore with birth-wet, wind-red faces
wiping the salt from our eyes
and notice sudden, welling
quiet, and how here the breeze
lets smells of growing things
settle and grow warm, a host of presences
drowsing, too fine-winged to see.

A green track, lined with meadowsweet.
Stone houses, ramparts to the weather.
Small fields that run all one way
to the sea, inviting feet
to make new paths to their own
discovered places.

After supper, lamplight
soft as the sheen of buttercups
and candle-shadow blossoming
bold on the bedroom wall.

Outside's a swirl of black and silver.
The lighthouse swings its white bird round
as if one day it will let go
the string, and let
the loosed light fly
back to its roost with the calling stars.

Christine Evans: Island of Dark Horses

Island Reflections

(Gerallt Jones spent a fortnight on Bardsey and during this period kept a journal. It was published in a limited edition.)

Monday, September 10th

The island has grown to be a part of my consciousness in a gradual shapeless way. I have given its contours and physical features comparitively little note, It is an atmosphere and a kind of cloak around me rather than a defined locality. And so this morning, when I wandered into the small enclosed ruin of St Mary's Abbey, it was the first time that I had really been aware of it, although it casts its shadow over my house, with its later Celtic cross, standing beside it, looming large alongside the path.

I cannot say that this remnant of grey wall calls up any particular visions in my mind. Whatever was the nature of monastic life on Bardsey, it was an inner strength that it must have developed, a resistance, a resilience, a tough interdependence that spread itself all over these fields, green from sweeping showers in the Dark Ages as they are today. It illuminated and informed every one of these four hundred and fifty acres; the stillness of their meditation was punctuated by the seal's mournful bark and the dry cry of gulls emphasised the silence. The most meaningful worship was the thankful seedtime and harvest that gave richness to these same fields, and their most meaningful protection and comfort was not any ediface of grey stone walls but the turbulent sea and the eloquent violent wind. They could climb to their ramparts on the slopes of Mynydd Enlli and lookout at the terrible dark world separated from them by the definitive barrier of Y Swnt; and from Pen Cristin on a clear day they could look south to that other embattled outpost behind the blue shadow of St David's Head. Standing within the shelter of the ruin, it seems no more directly relevant to the spirit that suffuses Bardsey than the fact that others have come to build houses here in this century, and that down by Maen Du there is a lighthouse that also stands out against wind and weather and shines into the dark.

Nevertheless, I felt this morning that the configurations of the place were in some way important. So I walked down from the abbey ruins, past Hendy, and wrote in my memory the feel and shape of things as I went. Everything stood out with a new definition, the solidity of the houses, Carreg and Plas Bach, their thick walls and geometric gardens, and the fade-away of the wet fields beyond, glistening with dew, stretching low to the little broken rocks where the seals lay. And on my left was a different picture, the steep sheep covered slopes, with Cristin within its seige-high walls and Ty Pella at the very end nestling in their shadow. The whole place seemed spacious, a big enough world, rich and full of minute variety. Crossing the tiny isthmus, past the landing-place, with the sea on either side licking submerged rocks, it had the impression of being new-made, unused, and I had the startling feeling that the grass I was looking at had never been trodden on. It was like a room with a new carpet, laid wall-to-wall for the first time. You stand at the door, momentarily afraid to spoil its texture, aware of its complete newness. Then the feeling passed and I crunched over dry sand towards the network of sea caves that finally face the stormy south. To create a way of life that was as confined as this, as structured and comprehensible, made a great deal of sense. It was a cosmos that could be recognised, treasured and kept in the mind, shaped and moulded and held all in one piece. It was a totality.

Each day the seals have been barking on the far shore, calling softly to each other through the quiet air and this afternoon for the first time I went close to them. I lay still on nearby rocks and watched. They were relaxed and at home,

their great calm eyes unafraid as they rolled over in the sun
and barked, out of no great necessity, but simply as a gentle
statement of identity. They could see I was there, but they
were unconcerned. They had no experience of human
danger, no need to scuttle back into the welcoming sea. This
strip of brown rock, camouflage brown, was theirs. But I
could come and go as I pleased. They would tolerate me
with no great interest, and watch me move off across the
warm afternoon fields with equal indifference. I read and
walked and loitered there all day with the seals for
company. When I occasionally spoke to them I received a
long still look of casual curiosity but nothing more. When I
finally moved off in the evening light, yellow across the sea
from the west, they didn't turn their heads or make any
significant movement.

R. Gerallt Jones (1934-1999): Bardsey

Enlli

No, I've never been there, with luck never shall,
Would be bored stiff in five minutes. All islands
Of this size are horribly alike, fit only
For sheep, saints and lighthousekeepers.
I've seen it at a distance from Aber prom
And that's as near, frankly, as I want to get.
I'm not surprised that hardly anybody lives there,
The gulls' gymanfa, the endless eisteddfod of eligugs,
The drooling chatter of the tide on the pebbles,
The moronic howl of the wind – well, I ask you.
Not, you'll say, much different from what goes on

On the mainland? Point taken. But
On top of all that, the traditions, paper flowers
Of crude fantasy, more than usually bogus
Even for this bloody country, if that's possible.
They had a king once, but he got drunk,
Well, that's kingly enough, but his crown
Was brass, he was appointed by the landlord.
And the gravestones of those twenty thousand saints
Thrown up in the age of faith by sheer ignorance –
Faith mostly spelt filth, futile pilgrimage
To no rational destination. I suppose that, really,
Is what Enlli is all about. You
My ancestors, were no fools who named it
One of the gates of heaven, outpost
Of the Kingdom of the Absurd, illogical,
Untidy, freak-out of geology, realm
Whose king had as good a title as some princes,
Almost, but not quite, nowhere, usually
Inaccessible but not always, utterly
Pointless but still marginally profitable,
Illusion, but anchored in rock.
If anybody prints this poem I'll send the price of it
To the fund to acquire Enlli for the nation.
God damn it, it is the Nation.

Harri Webb (1920-1994)

Winter at Harlech

This winter's day,
Closing down here now over cold and quiet Harlech,
Blinds the high catch of my evening nets –
Blinds the castle's eyes in sombre light –
As the sinking sun unreels the night
Where the long tides run, and time forgets,
In the love and shackle of my seagoing days . . .

And now the sky breaks to a dying flame –
The winter's turning in wheels of fire –
That stuns the harpooned sight,
As all the day begins to ebb and tire . . .

And time-worn towers, standing over sea and plain –
The granite pawns of a forgotten game –
Are caught by February fingers in trawls of mist,
Winding a frozen wake of winter pain
Where seas of clouds slowly tack and drift,
As I voyage for home and love again.

Bryn Griffiths

Seasky from Llandanwg

Such vistas, where the sky's colour
dissolves into the sea's, the sea's into the sky's
(most of all in an enigma
of azure, like today), the sense of boundaries
elides, and the horizon is
absolved of the necessity

of being, such vistas have a unique power
to haunt me, to pique with their ambiguity.

And should I be disturbed if a red boat
appears there, cutting a slow track
in the imperturbable sea?
The sea will close again, the boat
melt into the wedgwood, a black
hull infected with temporality.

Richard Poole: Autobiographies and Explorations

Penmaen Pool

(For the Visitors' Book at the Inn)

Who long for rest, who look for pleasure
Away from counter, court, or school
O where live well your lease of leisure
But here at, here at Penmaen Pool?

You'll dare the Alp? you'll dart the skiff?
Each sport has here its tackle and tool
Come, plant the staff by Cadair cliff;
Come, swing the sculls on Penmaen Pool.

What's yonder? – Grizzled Dyphwys dim:
The triple-hummocked Giant's stool,
Hoar messmate, hobs and nobs with him
To halve the bowl of Penmaen Pool.

And all the landscape under survey,
At tranquil turns, by nature's rule,
Rides repeated topsyturvy
In frank, in fairy Penmaen Pool.

And Charles's Wain, the wondrous seven,
And sheep-flock clouds like worlds of wool,
For all they shine so, high in heaven,
Shew brighter shaken in Penmaen Pool.

The Mawddach, how she trips! though throttled
If floodtide teeming thrills her full,
And mazy sands all water-wattled
Waylay her at ebb, past Penmaen Pool.

But what's to see in stormy weather,
When grey showers gather and gusts are cool? –
Why, raindrop-roundels looped together
That lace the face of Penmaen Pool.

Then even in weariest wintry hour
Of New Year's month or surly Yule
Furred snows, charged tuft above tuft, tower
From darksome darksome Penmaen Pool.

And ever, if bound here hardest home,
You've parlour-pastime left and (who'll
Not honour it?) ale like goldy foam
That frocks an oar in Penmaen Pool.

Then come who pine for peace or pleasure
Away from counter, court, or school,
Spend here your measure of time and treasure
And taste the treats of Penmaen Pool.

Gerard Manley Hopkins (1844-1889)

Hiraeth

The mountains braid the river
between moon-smoothed flanks,
groins, shoals of estuarine sand.

The Aberdovey lifeboat, a white gull
on the blue stream, crew staring down
as the three-coach train shudders through
and into the town where we once came
when our kids were small, hunting for crabs
under the pier, staying somewhere
in these stone streets...
                    All I recall
is the echoed distress of the gulls
at dawn.

The boy is dead now, the girl has
children of her own; the train pulls away
and I'm an old man, remembering
a land I'll not see again.

Selwyn Pritchard: Letter and Character
Comford Press, 2001

Sailing to Glandovey

One hot day we determined to try to reach our old friend Glandovey by water. While Arthur went down to the shore to see whether he could bargain for a boat, I cut sandwiches, hard-boiled two eggs, and put some tea in a bottle (wrapped in a rug to keep it hot).

'Let's start at once,' said Arthur on his return. 'I've captured a boat. 'The tide will be high about 4, and if we can reach Glandovey by 3 we can have our tea there and come back on the ebb. Now have you got plenty to eat in that basket?'

'Yes. I've put in enough for lunch on the way, and for tea when we get there. And I'm taking our sketching things too, as we shan't have to carry them.'

'And I got a bottle of beer from the inn. So off we go.'

However happy one's life has been, there are few days to which one can point and say, 'I would like to live that over again, exactly as it was'. But every bit of that day had either its fun or its thrill, both at the time and in retrospect. Mrs Hughes saw us off with some misgiving and urgent warnings not to be out late on the river. She was always full of warnings and misgivings, but she knew no more than we did of the difficulties in front of us. The Dovey estuary looks broad and inviting, as if butter wouldn't melt in her mouth, but she is a lady of moods and asks for navigation, not just rowing up and down. She has sandbanks always shifting, and we had to follow the channels that seemed best. When we came to a fine stretch of deep water, up would go our sail, and if there was the least puff of breeze how lordly we felt floating along for a while without effort. But soon would come a dead calm and sagging of the sail, or a sandbank and a struggle with the oars again. It was hungry work, requiring the sandwiches and beer.

As the river broadened out towards Glandovey the

sailing was easier, and we laughed at the train puffing heavily along, while we were gliding serenely, coming into the almost lake-like expanse of water near Glandovey. Here a tongue of wooded land stretched out into the estuary, and as we spied a convenient post for mooring our boat we disembarked, having a good hour in hand before the tide would turn. First of all we reconnoitred round for a good subject to sketch. Not that there was any lack of subject in all directions, but we had to find something we could manage. We had to avoid trees, and confine our attempts to the hills and marshlands of Ynyslas. We dashed the cobalt about recklessly and jeered at each other's results.

While Arthur was enjoying his after-tea pipe, I went down to the water's edge to see whether the tide had turned. Yes, it was an inch below the mark we had put, so I proposed our starting at once. Then came the best of the day, the tide and a gentle breeze both with us, and the perfection of Welsh scenery. A sandbank now and again would persuade us quite feelingly that we had better not linger, but a shove with an oar soon got us into a channel again. The tiller was hardly any use, for the wide stretch of water looked equally deep and our first notice of a sandbank was the actual sensation of the keel grinding into it. These banks soon became more frequent, and we ran on them so quickly with the breeze, that Arthur thought it safer to take the sail down – not so picturesque or so lordly, but safer.

M. Vivian Hughes: A London Girl of the Eighties (1936)

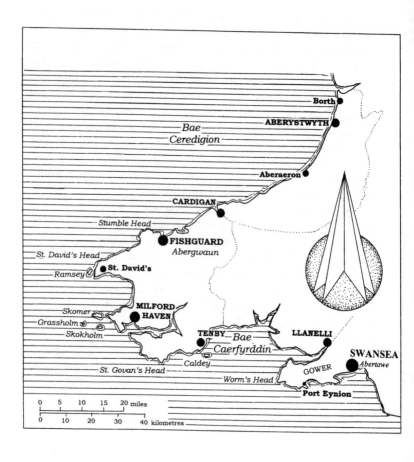

The Headland

Now from this headland watch the sea
With a dog's voice tearing at Cardigan.
Foul winds blow from Ireland and
Pile the bluff water, green weight and tooth,
On the sealed beach. The quiet drowned
Are tumbled in deep pools
Where ghosts of ships
Groan in their sandy bones
And holds of boulders.
All night long the crouching house reverberates
In the hollow vowels of the great winds.

Whenever the winds move they pull
Sea bird and land bird, gull and plover,
Away from their treacherous shelters, and toss
Such poor creatures tumbling that
Clouds lie under their claws.
Amazed, they see the waters hurled away.
All the waters of the world and all its winds
Roar blazing on this little coast,
On this small roof.

Latch down the cattle that the ravenous eating sea
Shall not invade them. Stones, hold down my thatch.

I lie alert in the great winds and walk at dawn
On this headland watching the sea
Gnaw at Cardigan. Tumbling like sacks
I know the drowned are in their early deaths.
Seven of this village,
Two straight men of my own veins,
Lie rolling in all the weight and tooth
Of these green waves.

I am an old and shifty poet,
Skilled in the strict metres,
I have need of my eloquence now.

Leslie Norris

Cardigan Bay

When in the whiteness of the sun the new leaves opened
    Through the face of your waters and pranced into the breeze,
    The juice of the spring returned tranquilly
To the trunk of each little wave; and the brushwood's
                      overflowing
Foam of buds whitened beside the meadows' hedgerows.
    And I would declare it was her spirit as far as the horizon
    Made you one milky growth; and her unseen phantom
Made you fresh and pure again. In the fold of your fields
She is my March, she my Cardigan Bay:
    She leaps through a head's heaviness, bubbles through
                     the veins,
Flings her flashing shoots across my dry rocks,
    Washes and polishes and brings forth her first fruits of brine
Above the unzealous sand. So, the race of men has not heard
    The equal of the spring that breaks from her border.

When on a sunshine day of spring your waters glittered
    With living mirth, up to the foam of the seagulls
    The brightness and blueness of splashes of driven snow
Insisted every minute it was my slender darling
Was the light and the breeze, and hers the thousands
    Of skies that deepened your depth. Their shadow came

Only from her bosom to me. I too am
Cantre'r Gwaelod, and through my cellars and cells
The waves that were hers spread through my halls.
    It's she swells under them, blows about me,
Swirling the sand and the gravel; surely it's her smiles
    Have closed round my doors, over my soul. I learn
Of laughs beneath the ebb and flow of their tranquillity
    I did not know of before in sickly merriment.

Bobi Jones: Selected Poems,
translated by Joseph C. Clancy

The Flooding of Cantre'r Gwaelod

There was another pause of deep silence. The noise of the sea was louder, and the gusts pealed like thunder through the apertures. Amidst the fallen and sleeping revellers, the confused and littered hall, the low and wavering torches, Angharad, lovely always, shone with single and surpassing loveliness. The gust died away in murmurs, and swelled again into thunder, and died away in murmurs again; and, as it died away, mixed with the murmurs of ocean, a voice, that seemed one of the many voices of the wind, pronounced the ominous words, 'Beware of the oppression of Gwenhidwy.'

They looked at each other, as if questioning whether all had heard alike.

'Did you not hear a voice?' said Angharad, after a pause.

'The same,' said Elphin, 'which has once before seemed to say to me, "Beware of the oppression of Gwenhidwy".'

Teithrin hurried forth on the rampart: Angharad turned

pale, and leaned against a pillar of the hall. Elphin was amazed and awed, absorbed as his feelings were in her. The sleepers on the floor made an uneasy movement, and uttered an inarticulate cry.

Teithrin returned. 'What saw you?' said Elphin.

Teithrin answered, 'A tempest is coming from the west. The moon has waned three days, and is half hidden in clouds, just visible above the mountains: the bank of clouds is black in the west; the scud is flying before them; and the white waves are rolling to the shore.'

This is the highest of the spring-tides,' said Angharad, 'and they are very terrible in the storms from the west, when the spray flies over the embankment, and the breakers shake the tower which has its foot in the surf.'

'Whence was the voice,' said Elphin, 'which we heard erewhile? Was it the cry of a sleeper in his drink, or an error of the fancy, or a warning voice from the elements?'

'It was surely nothing earthly,' said Angharad, 'nor was it an error of the fancy, for we all heard the words, "Beware of the oppression of Gwenhidwy". Often and often, in the storms of the spring-tides, have I feared to see her roll her power over the fields of Gwaelod.'

'Pray heaven she do not to-night,' said Teithrin.

'Can there be such a danger?' said Elphin.

'I think,' said Teithrin, 'of the decay I have seen, and I hear the voice I have heard.'

A long pause of deep silence ensued, during which they heard the intermitting peals of the wind, and the increasing sound of the rising sea swelling progressively into wilder and more menacing tumult, till, with one terrific impulse, the whole violence of the equinoctial tempest seemed to burst upon the shore. It was one of those tempests which occur once in several centuries, and which, by their extensive devastations, are chronicled to eternity; for a storm that signalises its course with extraordinary destruction, becomes as worthy of celebration as a hero for the same reason. The old bard seemed to be of this opinion; for the turmoil which appalled Elphin, and terrified Angharad, fell upon his ears as the sound of inspiration : the *awen* came upon him; and, seizing his harp, he mingled his voice and his music with the uproar of the elements.

His song was cut short by a tremendous crash. The tower, which had its foot in the sea, had long been sapped by the waves; the storm had prematurely perfected the operation, and the tower fell into the surf, carrying with it a portion of the wall of the main building, and revealing through the chasm the white raging of the breakers beneath the blackness of the midnight storm. The wind rushed into the hall, extinguishing the torches within the line of its course, tossing the grey locks and loose mantle of the bard, and the light white drapery and long black tresses of Angharad. With the crash of the falling tower, and the simultaneous shriek of the women, the sleepers started from the floor, staring with drunken amazement; and, shortly after, reeling like an Indian from the wine-rolling Hydaspes, in staggered Seithenyn ap Seithyn.

Seithenyn leaned against a pillar, and stared at the sea through the rifted wall with wild and vacant surprise. He perceived that there was an innovation, and he felt that he was injured: how, and by whom, he did not quite so clearly discern. He looked at Elphin and Teithrin, at his daughter, and at the members of his household, with a long and dismal aspect of blank and mute interrogation, modified by the struggling consciousness of puzzled self-importance, which seemed to require from his chiefship some word of command in this incomprehensible emergency. But the longer he looked, the less clearly he saw; and the longer he pondered, the less he understood. He felt the rush of the wind; he saw the white foam of the sea; his ears were dizzy with their mingled roar. He remained at length motionless, leaning against the pillar, and gazing on the breakers with fixed and glaring vacancy.

'The sleepers of Gwaelod,' said Elphin, 'they who sleep in peace and security, trusting to the vigilance of Seithenyn, what will become of them?'

'Warn them with the beacon fire,' said Teithrin, 'if there be fuel on the summit of the landward tower.'

'That, of course, has been neglected too,' said Elphin

'Not so,' said Angharad; 'that has been my charge.'

Teithrin seized a torch, and ascended the eastern tower, and in a few minutes, the party in the hall beheld the breakers reddening with the reflected fire, and deeper, and yet deeper, crimson tinging the whirling foam, and sheeting the massy darkness of the bursting waves.

Seithenyn turned his eyes on Elphin. His recollection of him was extremely faint, and the longer he looked on him he remembered him the less. He was conscious of the presence of strangers, and of the occurrence of some signal mischief, and associated the two circumstances in his dizzy perceptions with a confused, but close connection. He said at length, looking sternly at Elphin, 'I do not know what right the wind had to blow upon me here; nor what business the sea has to show itself here; nor what business you have here: but one thing is very evident, that either my castle or the sea is on fire; and I shall be glad to know who has done it, for terrible shall be the vengeance of Seithenyn ap Seithyn. Show me the enemy,' he pursued, drawing his sword furiously, and flourishing it over his head, 'Show me the enemy, show me the enemy!'

An unusual tumult mingled with the roar of the waves; a sound, the same in kind, but greater in degree, with that produced by the loose stones of the beach, which are rolled to and fro by the surf.

Teithrin rushed into the hall, exclaiming 'All is over, . . .

the mound is broken; and the spring-tide is rolling through the breach!

Another portion of the castle wall fell in the mining waves, and by the dim and thickly-clouded moonlight, and the red blaze of the beacon fire, they beheld a torrent pouring in from the sea upon the plain, and rushing immediately beneath the castle walls, which, as well as the points of the embankment that formed the sides of the breach, continued to crumble away into the waters.

'Who has done this?' vociferated Seithenyn. 'Show me the enemy.'

'There is no enemy but the sea,' said Elphin, 'to which you, in your drunken madness, have abandoned the land. Think, if you can think, of what is passing in the plain. The storm drowns the cries of your victims; but the curses of the perishing are upon you.'

'Show me the enemy,' vociferated Seithenyn, flourishing his sword more furiously.

Angharad looked deprecatingly at Elphin, who abstained from further reply.

'There is no enemy but the sea,' said Teithrin, against which your sword avails not.'

'Who dares to say so?' said Seithenyn. 'Who dares to say that there is an enemy on earth against whom the sword of Seithenyn ap Seithyn is unavailing. Thus, thus I prove the falsehood.'

And, springing suddenly forward, he leaped into the torrent, flourishing his sword as he descended.

Thomas Love Peacock (1785-1866):
The Misfortunes of Elphin.

The Land Beneath the Sea

What can you see in yonder bay
Save far-spread water at noonday
    Or boats, perchance, and ships beside?
But through the wave my glance is cast,
I see all as in ages past,
    The Lowland Hundred's pride –
The fair champaign, the growing grain,
    The royal park and smiling farms,
Each village neat and city great,
The plenteous harvest, boscage sweet,
    Both Art and Nature's charms.
Sixteen fair towns well fortified,
Surpassing all in Wales beside
    (Except Caerleon, the bright and proud),
All view I in their ancient dress,
Oh bright as song could e'er express,
    Where living souls do crowd;
All's clear to me as eye can see,
The vivid beauty of that land
Which you deem water, stone and sand,
    The Land beneath the Sea –
The deluged country song has hallowed,
In ancient days, Cantref y Gwaelod,
The vale at which the traveller wondered,
E'en Europe's gem: the Lowland Hundred.

Thomas Jeffery Llewelyn Prichard (ft. 1824-1861),
from The Land Beneath the Sea

Knock Three Times . . .

There is nothing of the rip-roaring gaiety at Aberystwyth that you get at Barry and Porthcawl. Even about the amusements there is a hooded, rather furtive look. 'Knock three times and ask for Charles Gee.' The dodg'ems are indoors and under cover. In the slot-machine section on the pier youths stand with a look of suspicious distrust as if the last commandment they had received on leaving home had been not to unleash a penny without consulting a deacon. Or it may have been that right across the road from the entrance to the pier is a theological college.

Aberystwyth seems to be a town mainly of old people. The front is a stretch of prim but gracious late Victorian hotels, hinting to roisterers to muffle their joy or get shot in the bay. On their steps a large number of people sit in the sun, knitting, stroking cats and not saying much. They may, indeed must, get rapturous climaxes of gossiping, but whenever I passed they were in this tranquil slough.

On the front's north side is Constitution Hill which crumbles from time to time and causes problems. The cliff railway takes you to the top of the headland. The entrance to the railway is red brick and lowering, as if Dante might have been a founder-member. The earth around is like the brittler type of biscuit. The view from the top is magnificent, shadowed only by outcrops of that flaking shale and the memory of the house at the hill's bottom surrounded by the rubble of subsidence.

There has been talk of driving a tunnel through the headland to link up with the bays to the north. Of this there can be little hope. It would take the most tactful type of mole to drive a negotiable hole through that material. From a distance the headland looks disturbingly like one of the older South Wales tips. I add it to my list of whimsical

Welsh hills that have taken a fancy to falling apart.

The beach lacks a rich sweep of sand. It is grey shingle crushed fairly fine by generations of holiday sitters. The sea moves very little this way or that, as if cured of all tidal frolics by the markedly earnest tone of the town. I would say that sitting on that shingle for several hours would make one thoughtful almost to the point of taking up Yoga.

Gwyn Thomas, from A Welsh Eye (1964)

The Birth of Venus at Aberystwyth

Beyond the pier varicose waves crocheted
A complex permanent nothing on the stones.
The Corporation deck-chairs flapped
Haphazard unison. Most sea-front windows

Confessed to Vacancies; and on the promenade
A violinist in Scotch-plaid dinner-jacket
Contributed little to the Welsh way of life
As he played 'Thanks for the Memory

To two small children and a dog. Without
Any expectation at all, the sea brandished
Its vanity. The one-eyed coastguard was dozing.
Nothing in the sky sought a response.

The occasional pebble moved, gave itself back
To the perpetual, casual disorder
Of all perfectly-shaped, meaningless forms,
Like pebbles. There was one beachcomber,

From Basingstoke, but he noticed nothing
Unusual either when far out, beyond
The beginning of the ninth (one could even
Go as far as to say the ninetieth) wave,

Dolphins who hadn't spoken to each other
For years formed squadrons for her.
Trenches of water broke open, deep
Where she was, coming up. Weeds fandangoed,

Currents changed their course. Inside
An instant's calm her hair began to float,
Marbling the hollows like old ledgers.
The sea still tells the story in its own

Proud language, but few understand it;
And, as you may imagine, the beauty of it is lost
In the best translations available . . .
Her different world was added to the world

As, nearing shore, sensing something dubious,
Something fishy in the offing, the dolphin-fleet
Turned back. 'The lady nearly drowned,
But hobbled in, grazing her great toe.

Do not ask questions about where she came from
Or what she was, or what colour was her hair;
Though there are reasons for supposing
That, when it dried, its light took over

Where the summer left off. The following Sunday
She wore a safe beige hat for morning service
At the Baptist Church. Even so, the minister
Ignored her as she left, and she didn't go again.

John Ormond (1923-1990)

Remembering Aberystwyth in the Thirties

The first thing I remember was the sea and the seagulls –
and thank goodness they're still there – thunderous roaring,
loud screeching and the wind slapping against my face. I
think this was after some great storm when my father had
taken my older sister and me down to inspect the damage. I
cried and wanted to go home to the Waun where the
elements were altogether less ferocious.

I wasn't very happy about a return visit to the town, but
it proved completely different; a rare afternoon of mild blue
skies and docile sea. And donkeys. Oh, the dear, patient,
plodding donkeys on the prom, some grey, some brown,
real eyes with eyelashes, fluffy round tummies, wispy tails, I
knew that if I could have one of my own I would be happy
for ever and ever, but my mother was adamant that it was
quite impossible: they belonged to the mayor and mayoress
of Aberystwyth and I was a very lucky little girl to be
allowed a ride on one, and please choose quickly because
they were waiting to be off

When you were three years old, all fringe, big eyes and
frilly dress, the boy in charge took your donkey's reins and
you rode in front of all the rest and it was the best time of
your life, with the salty smell of the sea and everyone

looking at you and you feeling like Shirley Temple or Princess Margaret Rose.

When you were four and there were smaller, daintier girls, one of those little creeps was chosen to lead, and you had to ride behind with the rest of the mob. It was a devastating lesson about Time's cruelty. I peaked at three.

Never mind, a donkey ride was still better than anything else in the world, far preferable to ice-cream, crisps or Milky Ways which were the other things you could get for tuppence, the extent of my spending power.

One unforgettable afternoon, an acquaintance of my mother's, seeing me still hanging about the donkeys long after my ride was over, offered me money for another. 'Oh, but she's had a turn,' my mother said. 'Well, let her have a second,' said this munificent woman – who wasn't even an auntie – lifting me up onto the nearest donkey's back. On such moments we catch dim glimpses of the Kingdom of Heaven.

I was never very fond of the sea, it was too sudden and splashy and to reach it required too much painful hobbling over sharp pebbles. Other more fortunate children had little rubber slip-on shoes for the beach, but my mother considered that stumbling over stones toughened the soles of our feet. And probably our souls, too. She was a daughter of the Manse.

Another thing I failed to appreciate was sand in my knickers. To tell you the truth I preferred picnics in a field, safely home in the Waun.

Siân James

Overnight in Aberaeron

Always a passer-through, because each place
One pictures perfect is unreal. Therefore
To stop here accidentally makes one a ghost,
Or makes each viewer of the place's heart
From hotel windows, immanent in it.
I lodge here who does not live anywhere.

Lads of the small-town plaza Saturday night
Shriek only, snatch delight and hurt not.
Tuned-up Hondas, but the curved coast road
Still fondles cliffs bent to its prickly screes,
The soil being prior to what we do to it.
We know such from these *windows*, nearly know.

Next morning, new names and a Water Street,
A harbour where to grind our heels from work,
From waves, from farming-sheds, from town, from tree,
From earth. Escape for all. I stow my sails
In mind, I self-deceive, look for what's ancient
In where one longs to live because one can't.

From this hill a yacht seems idle, saliently
Envisaging us idle as we fix
An eye without distraction on its sail.
A scissors-clip of white, a mile of blue.
Gulls taxi on the salt, incongruous cows chew.
I think the shoreline mirrors what I think.

Old inoffensive people walk to church
In gloves. Small boys dive off the quay.
The splash's hole refills, surprise gone quiet.
Pastel front doors beam fanlights round the square.
Each backyard has a laden apple tree.
The overfuelled technology's elsewhere,

The effluent it dispenses, din it makes,
The folk it educates and then corrupts.
We hear the noise of shingle, village grass,
The cool-spaced houses, owners having gone
(Bar those that die here or content stay young)
That everything may have its opposite.

While other things deny their opposite.
Hills cuddle houses, houses curve a bay,
It jells perfection. You leave this sort of place
Reluctantly, fearful to avoid
The evidently soft, the easy dream.
Starting the car, I go the ghost I came,

As though reality' stood out the same
Left to itself with some perpetual turning
Spade and fork, churning the earth. From there
The year's migration and the tourist's hub,
Re-surfaced road, approach road, lay-by, grab,
Earth-mover, mixer, four-mile jams of change.

John Powell Ward

New Quay

It takes about half an hour to drive from Aberystwyth to New Quay, on a road that runs like a lip along the coastline. Small villages look strangely toppled from a distance, their houses built haphazardly down to the water's edge. Even in genteel Aberaeron many of them face away from the sea, although they most often meet across squares and car parks. New Quay is different. Almost every single house there looks over Cardigan Bay with its windows opening out across the water. The spirit of the place embraces the sea.

According to literary historian David N. Thomas, Dylan Thomas's Under Milk Wood was to a large extent inspired by the time he spent in New Quay, and some of the memorable characters in the celebrated play, such as Nogood Boyo and Cherry Owen, are loosely based on colourful local figures. In his book on the poet and the environs which so influenced him, David Thomas carefully unpicks Dylan Thomas's wickedly inventive creations to reveal the New Quay prototypes buried beneath. The seaside village's newly-recognised place in literary history seems to appeal to visitors and locals alike . . .

When I go back to New Quay, I usually follow a very particular route. First I go to my grandmother's house high up on Picton Terrace. It was sold long since, but I can still stand on the road in front just as I did as a child and peer at Wales's highest mountain across the sea's expanse. I used to lean against the low wall for hours above the terraced garden of the house below and point a pair of binoculars through the palm trees and hothouse plants that flourish in New Quay's almost Mediterranean climate. The binoculars were my grandfather's, an old pair he used to take on sea with him whenever he went away. Like most New Quay men of his generation, he was a Master Mariner who spent months away at a time. When the sea farers came home they would bring exotic presents – lampshades decorated with ivory, chinoiserie, paintings, silks and even parrots. The attics of my childhood were littered with the spoils of British imperialist commerce. One distant relative even brought a slave home from the colonies, thinking that he could offer him a better life; they say that he ran off to London as soon as he could. As I stroll around the village I wonder if he ever found his way home.

Francesca Rhydderch in 'The New Welsh Review'
No. 62, Winter 2004

Llaregyb

First Voice

Stand on this hill. This is Llaregyb Hill, old as the hills, high, cool, and green, and from this small circle of stones, made not by druids but by Mrs Beynon's Billy, you can see all the town below you sleeping in the first of the dawn.

You can hear the love-sick woodpigeons mooning in bed. A dog barks in his sleep, farmyards away. The town ripples like a lake in the waking haze.

Less than five hundred souls inhabit the three quaint streets and the few narrow by-lanes and scattered farmsteads that constitute this small, decaying watering-place which may, indeed, be called a 'backwater of life' without disrespect to its natives who possess, to this day, a salty individuality of their own. The main street, Coronation Street, consists, for the most part, of humble, two-storied houses many of which attempt to achieve some measure of gaiety by prinking themselves out in crude colours and by the liberal use of pinkwash, though there are remaining a few eighteenth-century houses of more pretension, if, on the whole, in a sad state of disrepair. Though there is little to attract the hillclimber, the healthseeker, the sportsman, or the weekending motorist, the contemplative may, if sufficiently attracted to spare it some leisurely hours, find, in its cobbled streets and its little fishing harbour, in its several curious customs, and in the conversation of its local 'characters,' some of that picturesque sense of the past so frequently lacking in towns and villages which have kept more abreast of the times. The River Dewi is said to abound in trout, but is much poached. The one place of worship, with its neglected graveyard, is of no architectural interest.

Dylan Thomas (1914-1953): Under Milk Wood

Aberporth

Sky is performing feats of weather over
Hills wooded to the top, humped private hills
Whose birds look down not up. Briar's between
The fields: he keeps the eating sheep from knowing
What's on the other side. Beneath the path
A culvert tons, hidden for fifty years:
Some work will dig it up again.

Yes, nature is incurious, we know.
The butterflies as big as prayerbooks draw
No lesson from the india wings they thumb through,
While chapel slate aches with its uglification

Of primrose and violet, and the gold-black graves
Make even death elaborate and absurd
Like a bad conjuror.

The sea is much visited here, whose colours are cooler
And life uncertain as well it might be in
The earth's tears. Gulls on the sand look sharp.
Without anxiety the jellyfish is hideously still,
And the same could be said of the cliffs where wind carries
The loves of freewheeling crickets across a haze
Of sun-baked blackberries.

But we so easy are still not at our ease:
Such closeness open to us as though to a
Laconic Christ, hands flat to the ears with pity!
How we wish not to judge, wish for the starlight
And its emblems, the foliage globose and witchy,
With sounds coming nearer (Frrr! Frrr!) speaking
Of something that might content us.

John Fuller

Gwbert: mackerel fishing

The small boat lurches, drifting,
A low sun flares from the sea.
We offer them senseless bait –
Draggled feathers, bits of plastic.

First one or two bend the rods,
Are hauled in and neatly detached,
Then their ecstasy of hunger
Explodes against the lines.

Kamikaze torpedoes,
They take anything, bare hooks,
Clamp themselves on the crude weights,
Missing the lure, are hooked through the eye.

The lines wound in through clouded glass
Heavy with struggling silver,
We tear them from the barbs;
Jaws dangle, cannibal bait.

Spurting excrement smears the deck,
Hands smoke-grey with fish slime;
In cold fever they thresh in blood,
Gills pulsing like butterflies.

Going home, we butcher them.
Gulls' chaos of wings and hideous cries
Pursue the boat like furies,
Diving for mackerel heads and guts.

Silvered by the water's skin,
White bird *in* ice, feathered fish,
Shark's ferocity of appetite,
They swallow whole the offal.

Perched cormorant in devil's pose,
Nazi badge at sunset,
Squirts a scornful comment
On the horde of scavengers.

Days later we still pick from our clothes
Fish scales like flakes of mica
Clinging with mackerel tenacity;
Months after the oily smell remains.

Sam Adams

Walking the Cliff Path

1

As we climb, head and lungs clear,
The sky lifts, the blue-grey sea
Reflects a watery sun.

From cliffs with gulls below
The eye falls south, over
Arched, long-necked
Headlands, and returns
In a slow flight inland
From islands of volcanic rock.

Then the path descends
Into a hollow of gorse
And stonechats; heat brings out
The flies that love us; we clump
With skewed feet over stones.

2

At Carregwastad Point
We rest.
The 'last invasion'
Ended here, in drunkenness
And pillage.

Why here? Pen Caer
Was its own protector.
Still only' the sea wastes it,
And the acid lichen.

If I could paint
I would use its colours
On a surface of stone.

Blue-grey for the sea.
Green and brown earth colours.
Yellow for tormentil.
Red for the brick defences
Of a later war.

For the billy goat
That lives there,
Wagging his beard,
The colour of rock itself.

3

Some stones I return to
For those they commemorate;
To others for themselves.

We cannot read this one
To Dewi Emrys.

Your Welsh soon falters.
I stand monoglot before it.

And because we cannot read it,
We turn aside, listening
To a yellowhammer repeating
Its dry whistle on a thorn.

It is like a bird practising
To sing; but this is its song,
Ending always with a Tzee.

Jeremy Hooker: Pembrokeshire Journey (1980)

The Last Invasion

The French have come! They came in the guise of Normans, they came as monks to the monasteries, they came as Gascon knights to quell the Welsh rebellions, they came with ships and men to help Owain Glyndŵr, and in February 1797 they came in two frigates, a corvette and a lugger, under the command of a 70-year-old Irish-American, to launch the last foreign invasion of mainland Britain.

A small slab above the sea, a few miles west of Abergwaun, marks the site of this desperate enterprise. The invasion force consisted in the main of a thousand untrained convicts especially released from gaol, and dressed in dyed uniforms captured from the British. Its commander, William Tate, had been ordered to destroy the ports of Bristol, Chester and Liverpool, to divert attention from a proposed

French invasion of Ireland, but finding this task beyond his powers, he had decided to invade Wales instead, hoping that disaffected Welsh patriots would rise to his support. This was a mistake. The corps of criminals, once ashore, immediately set about looting, eating and getting drunk, never advancing more than a mile or two inland. The Welsh did *not* rise in sympathy. The ships hastily withdrew. Two Frenchmen were killed by a farmer and his son, another was run through with a pitchfork, and when the Militia and the Fencibles arrived in Abergwaun under the command of Lord Cawdor, after less than twenty-four hours General Tate sued for peace – as he convincingly explained it, 'the circumstances under which the body of the French troops under my command were landed at this place, renders it unnecessary to attempt any military operations, as they would tend only to bloodshed and pillage'. The surrender was negotiated in the Royal Oak inn at Abergwaun, where they still preserve the table on which it was signed, and all those scallywag commandos were imprisoned (though twenty-five of them, having chatted up some girls in Pembroke, enlisted their help in escaping, and in a stroke of brilliant impudence sailed away to France in Lord Cawdor's own yacht).

Jan Morris: 'Wales; Epic Views of a Small Country' (1998)

St David's Head

Salt sprays deluge it, wild waves buffet it, hurricanes rave;
Summer and winter, the depths of the ocean girdle it round;
In leaden dawns, in golden noon-tides, in silvery moonlight
Never it ceases to hear the old sea's mystical sound.
    Surges vex it evermore
    By gray cave and sounding shore.

Think of the numberless far-away centuries, long before man,
When the hot earth with monsters teemed, and with monsters
                                        the deep,
And the red sun loomed faint, and the moon was caught fast
                                        in 'the motionless air,
And the warm waves seethed through the haze in a secular
                                        sleep.
    Rock was here and headland then,
    Ere the little lives of men.

Over it long the mastodons crashed through the tropical
                                        forest,
And the great bats swooped overhead through the half-
                                        defined blue;
Then they passed, and the hideous ape-man, speechless and
                                        half-erect,
Through weary ages of time tore and gibbered and slew.
    Greyer skies and chiller air,
    But the self-same rock was there.

So shall it be when the tide of our greatness has ebbed to the
                                        shallows;
So when there floats not a ship on this storm-tossed
                                        westerly main,

Hard by, the minster crumbles, the city has shrunk to a
                                                    village;
Thus shall we shrink one day, and our forests be pathless
                                                    again;
   And the headland stern shall stand,
   Guarding an undiscovered land.

                    Lewis Morris (1833-1907): from 'St David's Head'

Porth Mawr

. . . one of the most ancient roads in Britain comes down here
to an open beach just above the rush and the roar of Ramsey
Sound and stops dead upon the sands. That open beach is to
this day called Porth Mawr – 'The Great Port'. The ancient
road here comes along the southern coast of Wales as far as
Carmarthen and then branches, one branch coming up
Cardigan Bay, which is called, I think, after St Helena, the
mother of Constantine, and the other coining straight along
by St David's. They call these old roads 'Roman roads', and
so I suppose they were, but still many of them were there in
some form before this island entered the comity of Europe,
before the Roman unity and order were finally imposed so
that England became England.

   Anyhow, there was a very old road of the first
importance, running down that way and near it stands the
see of St David. Now the interest is this: it comes down to
that beach above the narrow, roaring river of Ramsey
Sound. Why on earth does it strike the sea there? It's true
that antiquity pulled up boats on to the shore and might use
the beach as we today use a harbour – though in our tidal
seas a harbour was always better, I should have thought. But

even if they thought the beach better than a harbour (which it manifestly could not be for commerce), why should they call it 'The Great Port'? There it lies on a most impossible bit of coast, leading nowhere and as valueless a landing-place as you could get – granted a beach – anywhere in the island.

Hilarie Belloc (1870-1953): The Cruise Of The Nono

Ramsey Island

Drab gorse crouches;
and the stunted thorn, its back bent
from the lash, fleeing
the wind –
but root-bound,
like the girl becoming laurel.

There are no nymphs or gods pursuant
here;
barely a crippled tree is bared
against the sky.

Only wind, running
the turf one way like a close pelt;
and precipices to the sea.

Even men, who root anywhere,
landed, lasted a few brute seasons out,
were gone.
There is nothing to grip on.

* * *

The island's a bird sanctuary now.
Like the leaning wind, it has
prevailed,
becoming finally what it always was.

The once-gutted stone
habitation has been renovated for the warden.
With his deep-freeze, radio and books,
his sinecure's
as steady as a lighthouse job.
He'll last here longer than those
who had to, and couldn't –
each crude, repetitive meal
earned
singly, eaten
after darkness off the day's bare plate –

the fish-taste of gull-eggs;
a rim of chipped bone.

*   *   *

Cut off in winter
for weeks at a stretch, you hunched to stare across
the straits and see
a man ploughing a field dark
on the mainland in a cloud of gulls,
as if on the next hill.

Here the dirt was
thinner than the scalp on your skull.

But there were worse straits –
the rock was

fast;
you thought of those out in that running sea.

A fine day
was not a respite but increase of labour.

Yet there were the moments: going
out at morning;
the sea sometimes, when the back straightened.

In a bleak, intermittent
diary, kept a full year he survived
on the island, Ivor Arnold, poor
at spelling, and grudging
his entries
like flour or paraffin or twine,
recorded of a day in March, 1908:

'Wind S. A fine day. I could hear
Will Morris Pencarnan talking
to his horses yesterday from Congrwn Bach.'

Duncan Bush, from 'Saer'

Solva Harbour

Always one hill brilliant and one dark,
In memory – sharing the long curve
To sunset. Seas leap and fall
With a white sigh around two rocks,
Markers and exclaimers
Under whatever sky,
As we are ourselves

When we return, to breathe upon
Fading light. Is such remembering
A life form? Will it revive
Peripheral presences?
Floaters in the iris,
Vague to a central vision
Dazzled with happiness . . .

Forms we would now acknowledge, name
As witnesses: whether or not aware
On that day, how we sat stunned
In our own silence, like the boats
In the emptied harbour,
Waiting for inflowing tide
To move them again.

There was a girl running to swim
In the evening: she would be old now.
We scarcely noticed her pass
But the years insist, she was beautiful.
We would recreate her
Out of the mindless joy
Through which we sensed her . . .

She: and the flowers in our colours,
The seabirds. All we did not heed
Being on that day our own
Adamant life. In a sunned mirror,
Brighter than experienced . . .
Though it blows up for storm
And the harbour's grey.

Jean Earle (1909-1998)

Romantic Adventures

I met Martha just at a time when I was going right out of my way *to* meet somebody, one summer holiday in 1958, when Gus and I had taken the tent down to the Haven for just over a fortnight with the deliberate intention of meeting somebody, and of having the love affairs of our lifetimes. Anyway, the thing was that we got entangled with a crowd of Swansea boys, including, in particular, one hulking great pansy footballer of bronzed physique, called Dev, and in the end we got around to hating Dev's guts so much that long before the fortnight was up I had forgotten any randy impulses I'd taken with me to the Haven and was talking to Gus of spiritual elopements, wanting to succeed with Martha just to spite Dev.

By 'the Haven' anyway, I mean two tiny villages, Little Haven and Broad Haven, on St Bride's Bay, on the Pembrokeshire coast, and you may well not have heard of them. I reckon they're commercialised by now, but it wasn't too bad in 1958: there were a few people coming down from the Swansea and Cardiff areas for holidays, a few fields with caravans and tents, a weekly hop in the church hall, the odd camp-fire and groups of teenagers hanging around the chip-shop and the small café in the evenings.

This was the big attraction, of course. We were just about to go into the Sixth Form, sixteen and shaving, and now that we could go on holiday without our parents, we were all for going where the girls were. We dug out our scruffy old R.A.F. surplus tent, stuck it in Gus's old man's car and cycled down to the Haven. 'You wait, boy,' said Gus. 'There'll be some really nice girls down there.'

I suppose we could have done the job thoroughly and gone to Butlin's – a couple of the boys had – but, when it came to it, we liked the Haven. We'd been cycling down there for years, and when we were kids we used to get down there early on Saturday mornings in the summer term and fish around in the rock-pools for little creatures, anemones, starfish, small crabs, little worms, and sea-beasts we never bothered about finding out the names of. We'd collect these creatures, gather them in with seaweed of every kind, and put little clusters of them in jam jars to take home.

Sometimes I'd concentrate on seaweeds only, pink and brown and every shade of green. They'd grow, too. Put in a small pebble or two and the moss and the weed will grow on it, and the water will darken and grow rich. Then we'd worry that the creatures would die and would take the jars back to the Haven and empty them back into the pools. We were no biologists, but we did enjoy collecting those sea creatures. So, even when we went down that summer, we took a supply of jars along.

The first evening, though, all our plans were aimed at the romantic adventures of our corny young lives. We cycled over to the café in Broad Haven and, as we parked the bikes, saw three girls going in.

'Nice looking, boy,' said Gus. 'Look at that one with the pony tail. She's great.'

All our preparatory dreams brewed headily within us:

unattainable girls from Swansea or Cardiff, and wild ideas of their sophistication, guiding us skilfully into impossible amours. We were both, I suspect, slightly alarmed at the prospect and half-inclined to settle for somebody steady from Haverfordwest, but we didn't let on to each other.

There were strains of juke-box music wafting out on to the sea-front. The air was tingling with the sea-smells that had our hopeful senses jangling with a mixture of expectancy and panic. The music was pure syrup, rich, dark and lovely, a sort of cry-in-your-Coke country-and-western song, the sort of thing to madden any 16-year-old country boy with dreams of American mid-West farmers' daughters, sophistication and rich country pleasures rolled into one. We paused outside the door, very nervous now, because the great adventure began here. We went in.

It was a beautiful evening, in a tormented sort of way. We sat at one table, the three girls at another, a courting couple sniggered in the corner, and an old man who seemed to know the owner and have nowhere else to go sat in a cloud of pipe smoke by the door, passing the odd comment about the juke-box.

The girl with the pony tail *was* great. This was the age of the pony tail and the suntan, and she really was the country-and-western dream, hair streaming as she galloped on horse-back through my fevered imagination, or spun in a gingham dress through the mazes of a barn dance. I'd just seen the film of 'Oklahoma!' This was Martha and she really was Miss 1958. She was perfect, and I feared very much that she was beyond me, but went on dreaming just the same.

We did our best to start what our earnest minds pictured as a conversational rush. Gus fixed them with a weak grin and let fall a remark, unbelievable in its triteness, about meeting nice girls like them in a place like that. But they must have been used to this sort of banter in their own town, because they laughed politely and responded in kind. We kept up a fair conversation for quite a while on this level of crunching mediocrity, before we switched to the intelligent-discussion tack, considering the pros and cons of each record, for most of which Gus and I were paying, with rippling remarks like, 'Yeah. It's got a great beat,' each sharp judgment of this kind being pushed out to sage nods. It was a lovely evening. We didn't take them home or anything, granted. but we had just over a fortnight in hand and we knew our place.

We cycled back to the tent slowly, bemused by this vision of the bright sophisticated world east of Whitland. I think they were from Cefneithin or Llandybie or somewhere, but that, to us, was 'Swansea way' and made them virtually unattainable, giving us all the more reason for giving chase. We had no clearcut strategy – there were three of them to two of us for a start, and we both wanted Martha – but we had all the dreams in the world.

'Better keep those jam jars out of sight,' mumbled Gus, as we were about asleep. 'She'd think we were a right couple of dicks if she saw us fishing for seaweed.'

'Yeah, I suppose so.' I was sorry about that. I'd planned an extensive operation for the following morning. 'What'll we do?'

'In the morning? Play football.' That made sense.

Robert Nisbet:
from 'Jam Jars of Seaweed and Dreams of Love'.

Expedition Skomer

A boast of boys and a giggle of girls
in a boat off the higgledy piggledy coast
that wriggles through caves and coves and curls

to the waves of the holy bay of Saint Bride;
a boat that, perverse of nature, behaves
like a sliding, unstrapped saddle astride

to bottle-green, battle-bright hogsback sea.
So we rear our rocking-horse way across
from the wracks of Wales to the black bohea

of the bay of Skomer, the sea-green dome
of the pirate island with the cruel Norse name
where seals and smugglers have felt at home,

and Look! (shout the children) A puffin – there!
as we shrug round another shoulder of stone
and the sound of the outboard stutter and swear

as our heel splutters out, and the silken sand –
saffron and smooth – slides under the keel.
Then, praising God, I land.

                                   Raymond Garlick: A Sense Of Europe

Skomer Island 2003

The birds were shrieking and I thought of them
Down in those lank holes, with only their
Eggs to keep them company.
What did they say to them? Did they impart old knowledge?
Where are we to fly? When the Summer goes down.
And he said, out of the corner of the ear
There is a heavenly host of ghost riders on the plumes
Of wind worn currents. And there were white birds that
Should have been black, and black birds that could have
Been spirits. And in the night the shearwaters
Come tripping back on land in a midnight rush.
Harried by gulls, their big beaks, peck and slash
And the burdened body falls from grace,
Their weaning calls extinguished.
And all around, the skirt of teeming life
That feeds and flows and washes pain away,
The heavy oil that sinks to suffocate,
The faces and the flesh that bob upon the waves
The glittering gold of fish that enrich men
The rabbits fur that wisps between the bracken's fronds
The song of Lark arising up and up and angled down
To secure the hidden nest from prying eyes
The bowling bell, that Last of Spring's young fruit
The open vistas haunted by the barking, twisting owls,
The overturned and rusting gates, that lead to nowhere town
And life, replenished, succoured in its might
Cyclical and harboured, weaned, set free
To flight.

Sandra Jones

Skokholm

At dusk great rafts of shearwaters
Rise and fall with the slow tide
And the island's edge and colour
Lose definition. The wide
Fingered buzzard spirals down.
No wind sucks the sun-dried
Grass: the air contracts, still, but alive . . .

Suddenly the mist explodes, the sense
Is bruised by buffeting wings, the night
Is luminous with noise as bird after bird
Comes swinging home. I light
My torch, and catch one spread on the turf
Before its gull-proof hole. It hooks its wings
Arid slides below, leaving flecks of surf
To trace its track on the yellow grass.

In the iridescent morning air
Below the singing bird-shot sky.
Their sharp wings spread like arms,
The lost shearwaters lie
Eviscerated by the gulls.
Those without deep-shelters die.

John Stuart Williams (1920-1999)

Skokholm, A Challenge

In 2,000 years of history the little island had not ceased to challenge man, though it would be hard to define the reason precisely. To the older, experienced fisherman it was no longer very remarkable. Accustomed to live by oar and net, lobster-pot and sail, they saw the island with disillusioned eyes at last: to them it was only another lump of land breaking the horizon and the treacherous Atlantic swell five miles from their home beach. When young men fished there in those days of engineless sailboats, they were either more courageous or more foolhardy than their elders who fished nearer home. Courageous because although the catch was better the weather was a greater risk the farther you sailed from overfished home waters. Foolhardy because one day if you persisted you would lose all your gear – pots, nets, and lines – in the sudden storms which brought in the terrible groundsea from the illimitable westward ocean. Then the old men would nod: 'Aye, it always happens!'

But hope is strong in the youth of the heart. The soul of a young man yearns for the horizons beyond experience, the ecstasy to be unlocked over the edge of earth and sea. Hearing the fine tales of adventure related by the old men with sea-weathered eyes and long white beards, I learned that there were giants among them of olden time, whose daring spirit sent them forth to beat the bounds of the world, who rarely returned, but some were heard of as legendary figures, rich in possessions in far countries. A few, a very few, limped home in old age, the bitter secrets of failure hidden under the tawdry glamour of their natural garrulity.

Ronald Lockley: The Island (1969)

Pwllcrochan

I spent weeks down here:
Spring and Autumn planting and picking,
thick wedges of bread and tea,
hands smelling of earth and potato juice;
story-book childhood weekends of stolen
apples, blown birds' eggs, trespassing;
rainy evenings exploring the smugglers' cellar,
shadows jerked alive by the throbbing light generator.

The Old Rectory has gone –
scraped flat for a Texaco car-park,
abandoned after six months.
Now, outbuildings enclose a grassy space,
an ache of absence.
We walk the rutted lane to the bay:
from the narrow, stone bridge inland
the refinery spreads its shining tentacles,
its waste-burner roaring, glowing through the day.

The small bay is thick with reeds, wiry grass:
stream trickling over wellington-hungry mud
to slide beneath shells and sandstone shale
into the once-secret Haven.
Across the deep water from our fishing rocks
the gantries suckle from fat tankers,
steel arteries pulse away through the hills.

Looking back up to the road
I frame you in the camera lens,
centred by the cleft of the sloping fields.
You turn, Gareth smiles in your arms

and the photo worked perfectly,
bringing you into focus
and leaving all the rest behind.

As we walk back to the car, stepping from
bank to tussock, the marks of our weight in the mud stay,
draw an ooze of oil to rainbow our way.

Tony Curtis

Freshwater West

Over, break white and wash swiftly
Around this rock where earlier
Suds sand hiding swish and uncover.
Press, press on the slope of glass
Sliding over, over. White and pass
Me, wish peace and deliver
From hope, all you byegones, hush
And recover. Break ground and foam
Over and over, newcomers, beat
And surround, beat and surround
And repeat ad finitum, everyone
Beat till the few and the best of these summers
Of mine are as sand, over
And many and meaningless, far beyond
Hand and all measure, lost whereunder
Danger and no man's cast discover.

Wish. I am hidden already. Have I
A wish? Only for peace in the sudden
Hillock of glass and the green

Lease of the tide. Pass,
Pass on your way, over and over,
Beat and digress and repeat, young
Diver and mass old-white
With frays, press and retreat and recover:
Of your half wish there is nothing lost,
Nothing of praise and success, over
And over spoken, nothing but gland
And flesh, a rushing atomiser
Broken like sand from off the human coast.

Roland Mathias

At Bosherston Ponds

Near the ancient village of Bosherston on the south
Pembroke coast, the lily ponds are so old that no one has
been able to fix the date of their forming.

In November it is desolate, and distant
from the ruck of summer. The mashed carpet of leaves
lie apple-rust in the gravegaps,
their season done. Waves of high grass
wash about the church, drowning
the sunk mounds, the lopsided slabs
askew from weather and dying stock.
Names illegible beneath layered moss
clip me to futility, yet give that mild
pleasure we feel in cemeteries.
I am cousined to them by nothing
but a moment in Wales

and the loom of skulled union
under the roof of turf with the winning maggot.

History on this dot of the map
is sufficient to make me limp
a foot high. In my pocket a poem
shrivels to pinpoint. I look backward
for the peglegs hobbling
while I walk in cold time. I slither down
a long path mucked to a whirl of dung
and hang onto branches for support.

                          Solitary now
On a balsa bridge across the lily ponds,
I lose all strut.
Skidding along slotted planks, the bridge shakes
as my flimsy tenure shakes. I look out
at sheer rock and sloped dune, stretches
of water lily: something perfect occurred here
long ago, hacked in silence
without men or words – gaunt-winter-perfect
in frame of steel . . .

                          I turn back
up the steep track of churned cattle mud
where dead anglers trod, full of their hooked skill,
and riders stumbled, chasing a streak of vermin.
                          I scramble up
to slap of sea wind in my face
howling through the lost cemetery.
To the bang of winter, the coming events –
and the illusion of action.

                                    John Tripp

St Govan

St Govan, he built him a cell
By the side of the Pembroke sea,
And there, as the crannied sea-gulls dwell,
In a tiny, secret citadel
He sighed for eternity.

St Govan, he built him a cell
Between the wild sky and the sea,
Where the sunsets redden the rolling swell
And brooding splendour has thrown her spell
On valley and moorland lea.

St Govan still lies in his cell,
But his soul, long since, is free,
And one may wonder – and who can tell –
If good St Govan likes Heaven as well
As his cell by that sounding sea?

A.G. Prys-Jones (1888-1987)

Manorbier

Only about three miles from Pembroke Castle is the fortified mansion known as Manorbier, that is the house of one Pyrrus. The same man also owned Caldy Island, called by the Welsh Ynys Byr, which means the Island of Pyrrus. There the house stands, visible from afar because of its turrets and crenellations, on the top of a hill which is quite near the sea and which on the western side reaches as far as the harbour. To the north and north-west, just beneath the walls, there is an excellent fishpond, well constructed and remarkable for its deep waters. On the same side there is a most attractive orchard, shut in between the fish-pond and a grove of trees, with a great crag of rock and hazel-nut trees which grow to a great height. At the east end of the fortified promontory, between the castle, if I may call it such, and the church, a stream of water which never fails winds its way along a valley, which is strewn with sand by the strong sea-winds. It runs down from a large lake, and there is a water-mill on its bank. To the west it is washed by a winding inlet of the Severn Sea which forms a bay quite near to the castle and yet looks out towards the Irish Sea. If only the rocky headland to the south bent round northwards a little farther, it would make a harbour most convenient for shipping. Boats on their way to Ireland from almost any part of Britain scud by before the east wind, and from this vantage-point you can see them brave the ever-changing violence of the winds and the blind fury of the waters. This is a region rich in wheat, with fish from the sea and plenty of wine for sale. What is more important than all the rest is that, from its nearness to Ireland, heaven's breath smells so wooingly there.

Giraldus Cambrensis (1145-1223):
The Journey through Wales

Lydstep Caverns

Here in these fretted caverns whence the sea
Ebbs only once in all the circling year,
Fresh from the deep I lie, and dreamily
Await the refluent current stealing near.
Not yet the furtive wavelets lip the shore,
Not yet Life's too brief interlude is o'er.

A child might play where late the embattled deep
Hurled serried squadrons on the rock-fanged shore,
Where now the creaming filmy shallows creep
White-horsed battalions dashed with ceaseless roar:
Stirred by no breath, the tiny rock-pools lie
Glassing in calm the blue September sky.

Today the many-hued anemone,
Waving, expands within the rock-pools green,
And swift transparent creatures of the sea
Dart through the feathery sea-fronds, scarcely seen:
Here all today is peaceful, calm and still,
Here where in storm the thundering breakers fill.

Here where the charging ocean squadrons rave
And seethe and shatter on the sounding shore,
And smite this high-arched roof, and wave on wave
Fall baffled backward with despairing roar,
Or fling against the sheer cliffs overhead
And sow these vaults with wreckage and the dead,

Now all is still. Yet ere today is done,
Where now these fairy runnels thread the sand,
Five fathoms deep the swelling tides shall run
Round the blind cave and swallow rock and strand,
And this discovered breast on which I lie
Shall clothe itself again with mystery.

Lewis Morris (1833-1907), from 'Lydstep Caverns'

Caldy

Caldy's light works itself, throwing its message sixteen miles out to sea, white and red alternately, passing the nights in conversation with its brother, the Lundy light, across the waves to the south.

It has a splendid golden arrow shot through its cap, a weathervane, looking like the missile of some maritime William Tell. The cliffs are capped with slippery grass here, hanging in a casual fringe over the rocks. Seals lounge below, thick black seals, festooned across boulders, honking spectacularly, and raising their chins stylishly as the channel swell washes over them. There was a big one flat out across a single rock, lying like a man with a hangover, rolling a little to regain comfort after the passing of each disturbing wave. He gazed out to the world of blue-grey water, apparently decided it was all too much for him and closed his eyes for immediate sleep.

A seal family were busy in the waves just below me, jumping in and out as though a relative had fallen in and couldn't swim. Their heads bobbed comically from the water and they honked a lot. But the rest of the colony simply rested on the rocks, calling sometimes to reassure the others, but not bothering much beyond that.

There were gulls, of course, beating the blue sky, swooping against the rocky world, and making their lovely din. Their nests lie on the flat clifftop, wedged, but only just, laid out, displayed, as though awaiting the judging in some contest, each with its cache of spotty brown eggs. The gulls did not mind my being there by the line of nests, in their street. They stood back without anxiety, each bird nodding an exquisite head as though indicating its own particular handiwork. I walked along, inspecting them all, but keeping my hands in my pockets. I did not want any misunderstandings. Their beaks are like chisels.

At one edge of that far Caldy cliff there is an abrupt drop, and far below a massive oblong of rock, corrugated like a terrace, strikes out into the surf. It is like a skyscraper which has fallen on its side.

Look south from there and Lundy Island is a bruise on the distant, fading sea. East is Worms Head, a finger of 'Wales, west is nothing but ocean currents. Turn north, away from the cliffs and the seals and you gaze down the smooth green back of Caldy to the tangled trees in the valley and the toy spires of the abbey. It was very solitary for a man up there in the June wind, on the cliff with the gulls and the sound of the sea. A thoughtful place.

I stood, still as the lighthouse, and heard a booming voice. My mood told me it was the Voice of God, but it wasn't. Below, around the corner of the sea came a bright boat from Tenby, thick with trippers and a man with a megaphone drawing attention to the seals in the surf. Disappointing.

On the patch of green by the coastguard cottages I found Father Stephen. Some day visitors had just come ashore and two boys were kicking a red football across the grass.

'I suppose you could say that a man who comes here to stay sacrifices a lot,' nodded the monk. 'But I looked at the

145

world after the war and I knew that I needed something it could not give me. I've found it here on this island.'

Leslie Thomas: Some Lovely Islands (1968)

Praise of Tenby

I ask for God's favour, saviour of the folk,
Master of heaven and earth, greatly' prudent and wise.

There is a fine fortress stands on the sea,
The bright headland is gay at the Calends,
And when the ocean puts forth its might
Commonly poets are loud over mead-cups.
The hurrying wave surges against it,
They abandon the green flood to the Picts.
And through my prayer, O God, may I find
As I keep faith, atonement with you.

There is a fine fortress on the broad ocean,
Unyielding stronghold, sea round its edge.
Enquire, O Britain, who rightly owns it –
Yours, head of Erbin's line, yours be it now!
In this palisade were war-band and throng.
Eagle in cloud on the track of pale faces:
Before that lord and router of enemies,
Prince of wide fume, they drew up their ranks.

There is a fine fortress on the ninth wave.
Finely its populace take their case.
They do not make merry with taunts and sneers,
It is not their custom to be hard,
Nor shall I traduce their welcome –
Better a slave in Dyfed than yeoman in Deudraeth! *
Their throng of free men, keeping a feast,
Would include, two by two, the best men alive!

There is a fine fortress of revel and tumult
A multitude makes, and crying of birds.
Gay was that company met at the Calends
Round a generous lord, splendid and brave.
Before he had gone to the oaken church
From a bowl of glass gave me mead and wine.

There is a fine fortress on the foreshore,
Finely to each is given his share.
I know at Tenby – pure white the seagull –
Companions of Bleiddudd, lord of the court.
The night of the Calends it was my custom
To lie by my king, brilliant in war,
With a cloak coloured purple, having such cheer
I were the tongue to the poets of Britain!

There is a fine fortress resounds with song,
Where every concession I wished for was mine –
I say nothing of rights! I kept good order:
Whoever knows otherwise deserves no feast-gift!
The writings of Britain were my chief care
Where the loud waves broke in tumult.
Let it long remain, that cell I visited!

There is a fine fortress on the height,
Its feasting lavish, its revelry loud.
Lovely about it, that camp of heroes,
Is the wandering spray, long arc its wings.
Hoarse sea-birds haunt the crest of the crag.
Let all anger be banished over the hills!
I wish for Bleiddudd the best bliss that may be –
Let these words of remembrance be weighed at his wake!

Anonymous (c. 875), translated by Tony Conran

Tony Conran's note:
This has all the marks of being a dadolwch, or poem of reconciliation between a poet and his patron. The patron is a lord of Dyfed, or Pembrokeshire, called Bleiddudd; but the poem is remarkable among those of its type in that Bleiddudd is dead, 'gone to the oaken church', and the poet is making peace with his heir, the new head of Erbin's line, master of the 'little fort' – Dinbych or Tenby. If the last line of this translation is correct, which is open to doubt, it looks as though the poem was intended for recitation at Bleiddudd's funeral feast, at the November Calends, the festival of the beginning of winter. It is markedly anti-North Walian: Dyfed and Gwynedd must at this time have been at one another's throats. I have omitted the final couplet to God, and also a stray, fragmentary stanza that follows it in the manuscript.

More Than Pretty

The elegant houses of Tenby standing tall on the cliff reminded me of beautifully bound books arranged on a high shelf; their bow windows had the curvature of book spines. The town was elevated on a promontory, and so the sea on three sides gave its light a penetrating purity that reached the market square, and fortified the air with the tang of ocean-washed rocks. It was odd that a place so pretty should also be so restful, and yet that was the case. But Tenby was more than pretty. It was so picturesque it looked like a watercolour of itself.

It had not been preserved by the fastidious tyrants who so often took over British villages, the new class who moved in and gutted the houses, and then, after restoring the thatched roofs and mullioned windows, hid a chromium kitchen in the inglenook that ran on microchips. Such people could make a place so picturesque it was uninhabitable. Tenby had been maintained, and it had mellowed; it was still sturdy, and I was glad I had found it. But it was the sort of place which denied a sense of triumph to the person who secretly felt he had discovered it – because its gracefulness was well known, it had been painted and praised, it was old even in Tudor times, and it had produced Augustus John (who wrote about Tenby in his autobiography Chiaroscuro) as well as the inventor of the equal sign (=) in mathematics, Robert Recorde. But, then, there were no secret places in Britain that I had seen, there were only forgotten places, and places that were being buried or changed by our harsh century.

Tenby had been spared, and it was the more pleasing for being rather quiet and empty. I walked around dreamily. For the first time since I had set out on this trip I felt that a watering place was fulfilling its purpose – calming me, soothing me, making me want to snore over a book on a veranda with a sea-view.

Paul Theroux: The Kingdom by the Sea (1983)

A Tenby Childhood

Tenby's ancient name, Dynbich y Piscod, Tenby of the Fishes, would still have been appropriate at the time we lived there. The fleet of fishing smacks existed then and, in my opinion, were the town's chief ornament and pride; but now they have gone, and you look in vain for the russet sails of the trawlers in the Bay. What can have become of them I know not. The Harbour is now empty but for a few motor launches moored under the old stone pier. The tall plain houses above it, formerly yellow, are now painted white. The marble statue of the Prince Consort still adorns the Castle Hill: unmellowed by the years, it is as fresh as when it came from the factory. The rows of bathing machines which used to line the shores, and were hauled in and out of the sea by frantic men on horseback, are seen no more: these cumbersome adjuncts of a Victorian modesty have been scrapped. The town walls, or what is left of them, have not been demolished: an ugly and dangerous gap in the 'Five Arches' has even been restored and strengthened recently by a structure which, in imitation of antiquity, looks like a piece of cheese nibbled by colossal rats.

The band, which used to be engaged for the season, is no longer heard. In my time the principal social function of the day was the evening promenade on the Esplanade, the Castle Hill or the Croft. These rites, performed in semi-darkness or moonlight, with the sound of the sea merging with fitful gusts of melody, were calculated to promote a spirit of Romance and Adventure. Some of the members of the County Club, even, were impelled to desert their sanctuary for an hour or two, and mingle with the crowd in search of new sensations, or perhaps old ones. The annual influx of visitors presented interesting possibilities. The numerous caves below, easily accessible, provided privacy for those in need of it. But the retired Naval and Army officers seem to have departed, along with the orchestra. The town, in consequence, has lost much of the old diversity and style which the proletariat, now in occupation, is unable to supply.

Apart from the classy elements, the Tenby of my memories abounded in characters of a Dickensian originality. There was, for instance, Cadwalladyr, said to be the last of a princely line. This mysterious personage, tall, massive and hairy, enveloped in ragged oilskins, and up to his waist in the sea, seemed impervious to cold, as he pushed his great shrimp-net before him for hours at a time. He was never heard to speak, and perhaps only knew the language of his ancestors, which would not be understood in Tenby.

Augustas John (1878-1961): Chiaroscuro

Carmarthen Coast

Sea-hung cages of singing, hymn-barns
In villages of lace and brass and limewash
Look over the grey water. Held
In the lapse of a landscape's liquid outline
The islands float in air.

In the steep hayfields, in the deep lanes
Where the primroses linger till autumn
And the white trefoils star the hedgerow grass,
Where all the flowers bloom at once and forever,
You are near, but may not cross, the frontier of time.
Sweet heifers graze the saltings,
The tide laps at the roots of elder and thorn,
But the ferryman does not come to the ruined bellhouse.
You must stay
Or wander back to the parked car
In the lane that leads nowhere,
Gather the heavy blackberries
That grow only by this sea
In the queer light that shines only in this sky.
This is the edge of the world
Where you must mourn
For all you cannot escape from,
For all you have brought with you,
For Gwendraeth guilty with Gwenllian's blood,
For the silent sleepers under the green earth
Waiting, and waiting in vain,
For the named and the nameless,
For the smooth-tongued traitors and the dumb heroes,
For the white-robed riders by night
And the hands raised to curse at noon,
For all the starving ghosts and dead gods.
Fowls roost in tile chancel, nettles grow on the altar
Where the saints fasted and the pilgrims prayed.
This sea will not cleanse you, and there is no forgiveness
In all the empty sky.
You have brought no prayers, no tears. You must return
To the towns without laughter and the valleys without pride.

Harri Webb (1920-1994): The Green Desert

Laugharne

Off and on, up and down, high and dry, man and boy, I've been living now for fifteen years, or centuries, in this timeless, beautiful, barmy (both spellings) town, in this far, forgetful, important place of herons, cormorants (known here as billy duckers), castle, churchyard, gulls, ghosts, geese, feuds, scares, scandals, cherry-trees, mysteries, jackdaws in the chimneys, bats in the belfry, skeletons in the cupboards, pubs, mud, cockles, flatfish, curlews, rain, and human, often all too human, beings; and, though still very much a foreigner, I am hardly ever stoned in the streets any more, and can claim to be able to call several of the inhabitants, and a few of the herons, by their Christian names.

Now, some people live in Laugharne because they were born in Laugharne and saw no good reason to move; others migrated here, for a number of curious reasons, from places as distant and improbable as Tonypandy or even England, and have now been absorbed by the natives; some entered the town in the dark and immediately disappeared, and can sometimes be heard, on hushed black nights, making noises in ruined houses, or perhaps it is the white owls breathing close together, like ghosts in bed; others have almost certainly come here to escape the international police, or their wives; and there are those, too, who still do not know, and will never know, why they are here at all: you can see them, any day of the week, slowly, dopily, wandering up and down the streets like Welsh opium-eaters, half asleep in a heavy bewildered daze. And some, like myself, just came, one day, for the day, and never left; got off the bus, and forgot to get on again. Whatever the reason, if any, for our being here, in this timeless, mild, beguiling island of a town with its seven public-houses, one chapel in action, one church, one factory, two billiard tables, one St Bernard (without brandy), one policeman, three rivers, a visiting sea, one Rolls-Royce selling fish and chips, one cannon (cast-iron), one chancellor (flesh and blood), one port-reeve, one Danny Raye, and a multitude of mixed birds, here we just are, and there is nowhere like it anywhere at all.

But when you say, in a nearby village or town, that you come from this unique, this waylaying, old, lost Laugharne where some people start to retire before they start to work and where longish journeys, of a few hundred yards, are often undertaken only on bicycles, then, oh! the wary edging away, the whispers and whimpers, and nudges, the swift removal of portable objects!

'Let's get away while the going is good,' you hear.

'Laugharne's where they quarrel with boathooks.'

'All the women there's got web feet.'

'Mind out for the Evil Eye!'

'Never go there at the full moon!'

They are only envious. They envy Laugharne its minding of its own, strange, business; its sane disregard for haste; its generous acceptance of the follies of others, having so many, ripe and piping, of its own; its insular, featherbed air; its philosophy of 'It will all be the same in a hundred years' time.' They deplore its right to be, in their eyes, so wrong, and to enjoy it so much as well. And, through envy and indignation, they label and libel it a legendary lazy little black-magical bedlam by the sea. And is it? Of course not, I hope.

Dylan Thomas (1914-1953): Quite Early One Morning

Llansteffan

How still is the plaitwork of seagulls above the castle
As though for a minute they'd grown into the sunshine.
There'll be need to practise the presence of seagulls
To keep their light flight when they are no longer here.
My stomach warms to them.
They turn on their enchanting wings against the breeze;
They row, like a river I want to dip my cup in,
And all its feathers flow for my delight.

Memory of a castle, memory of a village, memory of people
                                        watching birds
And the Tywi rhyming grief upon its sand:
They caress the chime of worship yet do not disturb it.
An old pretty village where the whole world comes to retire.

And one senses the smell of ruin in the service:
Over there, crows repeat the tail-end of their hymn,
The tame attachments of their grandfathers' tidy customs
Veering before the skeletons of the recollection of yesterday
And the people below (are they preachers?) citing English.

Pure joy to the seagulls like angels in flight through the village!
Do they foster the old nature of the spirits of the buried life?
The sun is the lonely soul on their wings.
In a long graceful tremor they rain in a low circle
To whisper purity to the contemporary debris,
A flash of comforts before they climb on the back of the blue.
Oh! let care be taken to practise the presence of seagulls
To keep their light flight when they are no longer here.

                                Bobi Jones, translated by Joseph P. Clancy

Leaving the Beach

(Llansteffan)

She says 'It was always sad
leaving the beach'. On those distant holidays
she knew we'd be back by the sea next day,
yet it didn't feel safe
packing towels and spades,
abandoning our sandcastle,
forcing on gritty shoes
to plod back to the hot car.
She had no words to say
how final each day's leaving felt,
or how it seemed a foretaste.

A rainy year has conceded, late,
a few hours of summer. We sit
above the beach. Her smile forgives
sun that raced west, sandcastle drowned,
these gulls that sound the same.

Ruth Bidgood: Singing To Wolves

Burry Holm

Sitting cross-legged on a cliff on Burry Holm,
open to the wind and the wide sea,
faced with the endlessly modulating greys,
you point in delight at the fulmars
that are planing past on their stiff wings.

Southward, the Worm is pulling strongly out to sea,
but held by the tail's still stationary.
The jagged curves of surf in Rhossili bay,
the concussive circles of the waves,
repeat their indefinite invasions of the beach.

While the ragged discs of the golden lichen Xanthoria,
encrusting the cliff like memorial Celtic suns,
emblazon echoes on the stones. You run
your hands over the radiant Braille of their faces.
'Don't you see' you say, as you sway in the west wind,

'the blinding sun that shines beyond the greys?'

Don Rogers

Snaps at Gower 1933

1

Three apprentices
posing like strongmen in the shallows:
one with shoulder straps and pot, grinning a Colgate grin;
one, pigeon-chested, serious:
both sparsely-tanned and tall, my short-arse father
sandwiched in between.
A fine summer's day: behind them – cliff and sky
and frolicking surf. Out of frame:
three girls giggling, faraway Works and Town
gently dozing in the sepia afternoon

heart-throbs! Three gallants:
    s out and stomachs in
a.. s firmly folded for posterity
as though Beach-Bully Time
could never kick the sand
into their eyes

2

Five on a lone promonotory:

laughing and saying cheese
arms around shoulders linked:
my mother bath-robed, hair all wet.
three other girls: two quite nice-looking wearing shorts,
one fat and twenty on the end and fully-dressed.
All four support my father – a trainee gigolo,
sleek swim-suited, legs like Nureyev.
High tide, almost. I do not recognize the rock
or the distant strip of drab peninsula.
Their clothes lie scattered.
Soon they must hurry and dress
before they get cut off . . .

3

Four crouching in mill-pond water:
blur of a cliff behind and minute bathers.
Sunlight. Warmth shining through
each fingerprint and tear
and full discoloration.
Four grins dissolving as one in radiating ripples.

Alan Perry

On the Finger-tip of Gower

I walked westwards along the sunlit cliffs of Gower. A blue sea flowed to meet shining headlands and swept foaming into the bays between them. Over the Severn Sea white clouds raced out towards Devon. I came to Oxwich, beautiful for the limestone buttresses of its cliffs. Buzzards switchbacked in the high winds, ravens croaked over the woods and a peregrine passed like an arrow. Here that delight among ferns, the rusty-back, adorned the crevices. Oxwich bay and dunes were now below me: a scene of infinite peace that mid-March day. I was grateful to see it so early in the year for this is a very popular holiday haunt later on.

After Oxwich I let the main road lead me inland and back again to the coast near Paviland Cave, where the skeleton of 'The Red Lady' was found by Dr William Buckland in 1823 and which is amongst our most cherished palaeolithic specimens. I had now reached one of the choicest parts of Gower; those altogether delightful, flat-topped Paviland cliffs that ask to he walked along or leapt along in the company of sea winds, gulls and the scent of gorse.

The tide was in and the caves wave-spumed and inaccessible. But did that matter? Sufficient to have savoured these earliest haunts of man, to have got the feel of this ancient place, to have sat in the sun and imagined past scenes when the air was frigid, the sea further away and the caves looked out from a dry, raised platform onto an Arctic world which Paviland man shared with woolly rhinoceros, reindeer and other beasts whose bones were found with his in the caves. That day, as I looked across Gower to the shining snowfields of upland Carmarthenshire, the Arctic did not seem to have retreated very far.

But from these Paviland cliffs it is not to the north that

you most naturally look. It is the west which pulls you, for now you see to the end of the peninsula. There is just enough curve in the coast to give you a glimpse of Worm's Head where it wriggles into the sea several miles away. And now if you want as heart-lifting a cliff-path as you could desire you may walk those last miles to the end of Gower. Here in summer you may find a choice collection of limestone plants, including the very rare small restharrow, the equally rare goldilocks, the hoary rockrose and the spiked speedwell: all good reasons for making these cliffs worthy of their status of National Nature Reserve.

William Condry (1918-1998): Welsh Country Essays

Port Eynon

To arrive mid-morning, the very wide curve
Of the bay receding and maybe sixty persons
In its vision of nearly two miles. They swim
(Cold getting in; it warms, the blood warms next
Like lemons and tomatoes) and the sun's orange
Fails – just – to break through. Sand
Has been dredged from the shore, they said,
To make buildings and roads, but still by noon
A hundred people are walking, then swimming, there.

The trunks, the costumes, the clothes. Blue
As frequent as the sea and purple like far
To the horizon: green and yellow as the buoys.
Shaggy blacks and greys adorn or stretch tight
On stomachs and hearts, not shoulders though

For sun or the back of the head (for all look out
To that far grey-blue). At one o'clock a couple
Of hundred wives, tanned old men with white
Hair, children of every mien and size, are there.

When the sun, at last emerging, carefully sweeps
The final bits and flurries of cloud away, the edge
Of the flat sea speckles with splash, shouts
And some distant laughter. Two toddlers
Wield their spades as though a motorway
Slip road depended on it, and a beach ball
Bobs from hairy head to sun hat to balding pate
In a curious mix of tall and dazed activity;
Slowing somewhat, as the heat soothes and slows.

Three p.m; four hundred people surely,
Thirty or so in a few speedboats which shoot
In a loud thin drone out to sea, out of sight,
Never to return it seems, but no one cares,
As row on row of torsos statuesque,
Waist-high visible, in twos or threes or alone,
Face the same outward direction. Behind
On very dry sand, scalded weed and
Mother-of-pearl, so many more doze or sleep.

I can't record, how they darken as they distance,
The ochre sun and the blending cerulean blue
Behind them to throw small innocent shadows. Here
Is a populous mysticism, somehow a rite
Shimmeringly performed; even the border collies
Know just how to race in exact parallel
To the shore's pebbly line. Buckets propel
The inchy streams round dams into kid-made pools
Where frowning babies are sat, their dads unalarmed.

At five o'clock, or six, or eight, it is silently
Felt that all, us all, have unwittingly passed by
Some moment of consummation: an entire
Caravan park as if baptised. Some leave for home,
Then more; last swims are indulged or cooler
Hazarded; the water is stroked; light fades a little
But not the surface of the sea, flat as even
It was at first morning. When we left, some stayed,
Liking as much the gentling grey, and dusk.

John Powell Ward

A Walk by the Sea

This morning we drove to the Mumbles, the Westhorps, Miss Brown and myself. As we went through lovely Sketty where Welby was Vicar for fourteen years we stopped to look at the Church and Churchyard. The Church is nice but the lychgate is desecrated by the names of all the snobs of Swansea.

A tramway runs along the road side from Swansea to the Mumbles, upon which ply railway carriages drawn by horses.

Oystermouth Castle stands nobly upon a hill overlooking the town and bay. The lurid copper smoke hung in a dense cloud over Swansea, and the great fleet of oyster boats under the cliff was heaving in the greenest sea I ever saw. We had luncheon upon the Cliffs overlooking the white lighthouse tower upon the most seaward of the Mumbles. A shepherd was holloing and driving the sheep of the pasture furiously down a steep place into the sea, and a school of boys came running down the steep green slope, one of them playing 'Rosalie the Prairie Flower' on an accordion as he ran. A steam tug shot out of Swansea Harbour to meet a heavily laden schooner under full press of canvass in the bay and towed her into port, and the great fleet of oyster boats which had been out dredging was coming in round the lighthouse point with every shade of white and amber sails gay in the afternoon sun as they ran each into her moorings under the shelter of the great harbour cliff. As we went along the narrow Cliff path among the gorse towards Langland and Caswell Bay, a flock of strange and beautiful black and white birds flew along the rock faces below us towards the lighthouse piping mournfully. They were I suppose a small kind of gull but they seemed to me like the spirits of the shipwrecked folk seeking and mourning for their bodies. Among the sighing of the gorse came upon a lift of the wind a faint and solemn tolling of a deep bell from seaward. It was the tolling of the buoy bell moored off the Mumbles, a solemn awful sound, for the bell seemed to be tolling for the souls of those who had gone down at sea and warning the living off their graves.

Francis Kilvert (1840-1879): Diary

Llanmadoc Down

I have the contours and face by heart
stacked stones and circles of the iron age fort
scrolled bracken and red earth
know from every point of my compass
assuming each weather's fashion
to try the styles of a cold passion

woaded heather or russet bracken
compose hearts' blood-lapse
colouring griefs and births
sea-fog and moonless night figure emptiness
warm renewals of embrace
glint in the never out of season gorse

we scramble for a spring day in Rhossilli
climb down to Bluepool at August's low tide
rainproofs round waist and pockets of picnic
first-foot the highest ridge to sight Worms Head
January sunset dipping red
stage our seasons' story

days you must take ocean on trust
viewing gaps fill up with mist
moralise crag and cairn
catch breath when larks wind up an air
fox runs or rooks fly at a sparrowhawk
shine on sea-edge maps peninsula

but to observe the foursquare tormentil
lamb's bleached ribcage on the hill
or fingered scrawls in piled limestone
is to feel the hill's creatures hold their own
as when we form the manshape from a name
new stars move in to discompose the frame.

Barbara Hardy:
Severn Bridge: New and Selected Poems

Ode to Swansea

Bright town, tossed by waves of time to a hill,
Leaning Ark of the world, dense-windowed, perched
High on the slope of morning,
Taking fire from the kindling East:

Look where merchants, traders, and builders move
Through your streets, while above your chandlers' walls
Herring gulls wheel, and pigeons,
Mocking man and the wheelwright's art.

Prouder cities rise through the haze of time,
Yet, unenvious, all men have found is here.
Here is the loitering marvel
Feeding artists with all they know.

There, where sunlight catches a passing sail,
Stretch your shell-brittle sands where children play,
Shielded from hammering dockyards
Launching strange, equatorial ships.

Would they know you, could the returning ships
Find the pictured bay of the port they left
Changed by a murmuration,
Stained by ores in a nighthawk's wing?

Yes. Through changes your myth seems anchored here.
Staked in mud, the forsaken oyster beds
Loom; and the Mumbles lighthouse
Turns through gales like a seabird's egg.

Lundy sets the course of the painted ships.
Fishers dropping nets off the Gower coast
Watch them, where shag and cormorant
Perch like shades on the limestone rocks.

You I know, yet who from a different land
Truly finds the town of a native child
Nurtured under a rainbow,
Pitched at last on Mount Pleasant hill?

Stone-runged streets ascending to that crow's nest
Swinging East and' West over Swansea Bay
Guard in their walls Cwmdonkin's
Gates of light for a bell to close.

Praise, but do not disturb, heaven's dreaming man
Not awakened yet from his sleep of wine.
Pray, while the starry midnight
Broods on Singleton's elms and swans.

Vernon Watkins (1906-1967)

A Cold White Day in Swansea

It was a cold white day in High Street, and nothing to stop
the wind slicing up from the docks, for where the squat and
tall shops had shielded the town from the sea lay their
blitzed flat graves marbled with snow and headstoned with
fences. Dogs, delicate as cats on water, as though they had
gloves on their paws, padded over the vanished buildings.
Boys romped, calling high and clear, on top of a levelled
chemist's and a shoe-shop, and a little girl, wearing a man's

cap, threw a snowball in a chill deserted garden that had once been the Jug and Bottle of the Prince of Wales. The wind cut up the street with a soft sea-noise hanging on its arm, like a hooter in a muffler. I could see the swathed hill stepping up out of the town, which you never could see properly before, and the powdered fields of the roofs of Milton Terrace and Watkin Street and Fullers Row. Fish-frailed, netbagged, umbrella'd, pixie-capped, fur-shoed, blue-nosed, puce-lipped, bunkered like drayhorses, scarved, mittened, galoshed, wearing everything but. the cat's blanket, crushes of shopping-women crunched in the little Lapland of the once grey drab street, blew and queued and yearned for hot tea, as I began my search through Swansea town cold and early on that wicked February morning. I went into the hotel. 'Good morning.'

The hall-porter did not answer. I was just another snowman to him. He did not know that I was looking for someone after fourteen years, and he did not care. He stood and shuddered, staring through the glass of the hotel door at the snowflakes sailing down the sky, like Siberian confetti.

Dylan Thomas (1914-1953): Return Journey
from 'Quite Early One Morning'

Swansea Bay

There is the whiff of death
on the breadth of your surf,
the ebb and flow of smashed dreams.

Like so many of your lovers
I am appalled and thrilled by you.

Each wave bounds in
with the complex mix
of decay and liberty

the sun on your rim
reminds me of those
who crossed the sometime
calm of your watery palm
to build and fulfil their dreams

yet with the crash, smash and boom
of your arrival at my feet

I know you will turn on the wind
from servant to tyrant.

Peter Read

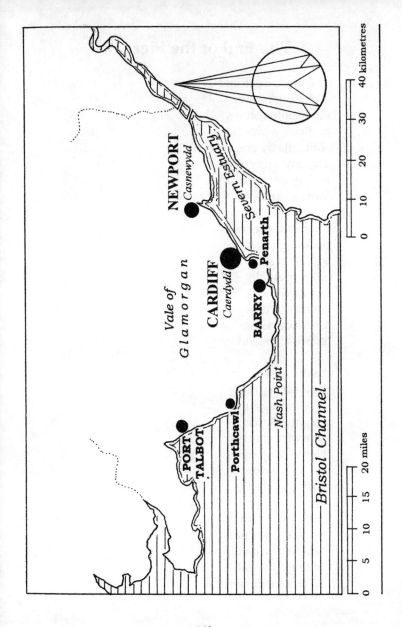

169

The End of the Pier

The pressure drops.
– Missing the sun
bay-fronted shops
on Bryn-y-Mor Rd
shut, one by one.
The day's forgotten
fruit goes rotten.
Yawns explode.

That stuff the sea
packs tightly in
a chest of sand
. . . perpetually
and anyhow . . .
resurfaces now
as clouds begin
to cross the land.

All over town
dusk catalogues
the washing-lines
weighed down
by tearful sheets,
the one-way signs,
and all the dogs'
examined streets.

– However slow
they are, days pass
and, every night,
looking for a ball
lost in long grass

thirty years ago,
the lighthouse light
finds nothing at all

along the coast
except for starfish
the waves discard –
giving up the ghost
until they're hard
enough to wish
upon – and then
the pier again.

My pockets are full
of pennies and sand.
A tugboat, I take
my daddy's hand.
I pull and I pull,
because he turns so
slowly in my wake,
and won't let go.

Stephen Knight

In Port Talbot

By now it's like returning to a foreign town, especially
at night when the steelworks' odd familiar fever
flushes again faint red on walls and ceilings.
Its reverberations, too, this time I cannot hear
as silence. When cars stop smashing rain to spray
or after a train has dragged its chain across stone floors
what remains is this, work's dying murmur.

Lying flat, the whole town breathes through stacks;
gouts of asthmatic coughing churn the sky.
All night in burnt air, an enormous radio
aglow with coiled circuits, aerials straining high,
blasts out selections from Smoke at ranked streets
with floatings of thick chords that echo for miles.
They drown, almost, the groundswell hum nearby.

Homes of the well-off on Pentyla have the best view
of the steelworks. The main road follows it obediently.
Running coastwards greased by rain, streets skidded
to this edge, finding metal had replaced the sea
with slabs that rear white-ridged with steam then stop.
All night, rolling in over the beached town
are breakers never seen, a thrumming like memory.

Look out on winter's thin streets. See how steel
lights up the whole town still. Although it shivers now
in November dreaming of steel's breaking point, its people –
kept from clean air but not each other – could tell how
common purpose, gathering, runs strongest
on hardest ground. As here where the land turned
overnight to metal, where smoke blooms in the window.

And when at last shared work's vibrations cease,
sharing itself will fade (as the mining villages nearby)
with Keir Hardie's dream, with Bethanias long since ghosts,
down history's shaft. Difference and indifference will untie
taut bonds of work that cramp yet forged here a community;
then old South Wales will have to start a New. Meanwhile
reverberations still, slow leavings, long goodbye.

John Davies

Heron at Port Talbot

Snow falls on the cooling towers
delicately settling on cranes.
Machinery's old bones whiten; death
settles with its rusts, its erosions

Warming of winds off the sea
the motorway dips to the dock's edge.
My hands tighten on the wheel against
the white steel of the wind.

Then we almost touch, both braking flight,
bank on the air and feel that shocking
intimacy of near-collision,
animal tracks that cross in snow.

I see his living eye, his change of mind,
feel pressure as we bank, the force
of his beauty. We might have died
in some terrible conjunction.

The steel town's sulphurs billow
like dirty washing. The sky stains
with steely inks and fires, chemical
rustings, salt-grains, sand under snow.

And the bird comes, a surveyor
calculating space between old workings
and the mountain hinterland, archangel
come to re-open the heron-roads,

meets me at an inter-section
where wind comes flashing off water
interrupting the warp of snow
and the broken rhythms of blood.

Gillian Clarke

A Fascinating Stretch of Territory

The country around Porthcawl is as fascinating a stretch of
territory as you will find in the land. It is lapped in legend
and lollies, warm with old romance and endless tea-urns.
Joy with a widening wake of wafers.

Stand on the edge of Rest Bay and your eye can look on
as vivid a contrast of scene and historic meaning as you can
ever wish. To the left, way beyond the teeming sand-
dwellers at Trecco Bay, is the curl of clifftop turf at
Southerndown where once the wreckers of Dunraven plied
their odd trade of swinging crafty lanterns to lure ships on
to the rocks. They are gone, and the outfall at Ogmore is left
to keep the balance of history right. To the west is that
coastal strip of massive mills and dakening skies.

As a child I remember that one of the many moot points which kept the chapel elders in a constant state of feud was whether the annual treat should go to Barry Island or Porthcawl. Barry usually won. It was nearer. We felt more at home in the loose, lusty jacket of Whitmore Bay. Besides there was a suggestion of tone, dignity, even coldness about Porthcawl. The word 'Rest' always settled uneasily on creatures whose one aim in life was to deafen the world with the din of their delight.

And there was the matter of the wind. A gale seemed in those years to have got itself lost on Lock's Common. There was a tale told of a miner, enfeebled by illness and overwork to the lowest point of vitality. He went to the Miners' Rest at a time when the autumn gales were going into dress-rehearsal and they got the man well between their sights. Unless he had his stick driven six inches into the ground and a private tree to act as a windbreak, he could not stand erect. On his return to the Rest each day he had to be treated for excess air. But he was told: 'That's the beauty of the place, that's the value. It's so bracing.' The wind raced to a climax. He was picked up by a gust from Mumbles way one day and hurled against the rock face. He broke a collarbone but all he did was to get up and say, 'By God, it's bracing, like they said!'

Gwyn Thomas (1913-1981): A Welsh Eye

At Ogmore-by-Sea This August Evening

I think of one who loved this estuary –
my father – who, self-taught, scraped upon
an obstinate violin. Now, in a room
darker than the darkening evening outside,
I choose a solemn record, listen to
a violinist inhabit a Bach partia.
This violinist and violin are unified.

Such power! The music summons night. What more?
It's twenty minutes later into August
before the gaudy sun sinks to Australia.
Now nearer than the promontory paw
and wincing electric Porthcawl
Look! The death-boat black as anthracite,
As its spotlit prow a pale familiar.

Father? Here I am, Father. I see you
jubilantly lit, an ordered carnival.
The tide's in. From Nash Point no foghorns howl.
I'm at your favourite place where once you held
a bending rod and taught me how to bait
the ragworm hooks. Here, Father, here, tonight
we'll catch a bass or two, or dabs, or cod.

Senseless conjuration! I wipe my smile away
for now, lit at the prow, not my father
but his skeleton stands. The spotlight fails,
the occult boat's a smudge while three far lighthouses
converse in dotty exclamation marks.
The ciaccona's over, the record played,
there's nothing but the tumult of the sea.

Dannie Abse: New and Collected Poems (2003)

A Jekyll and Hyde Town

Barry Island has been the jewelled eye in the childhood summers of millions of us, and from its docks has poured a quantity of coal large enough to have left at least three mountains in the north of the county quite hollow. There are few South Walians for whom Whitmore Bay and Bindles Ballroom have not furnished some hook of memory on which to hang a pleasant, evening thought.

Barry is, of course, a Jekyll and Hyde town. It developed rapidly into one of the finest Welsh ports, and it also had a stretch of sand that gave it glamour of Bali for the herded troglodytes dreaming of the sea in the austere terraces of the valleys to the north. Now the docks have passed their zenith of wealth and power. The amount of coal passing through the dock gates would just about keep a vestry warm.

These facts have limelit the question of how much Barry should do to develop, consciously and expertly, its advantages as a resort. The debate is constant in the town and it evokes a good deal of eloquence and bad temper. The first essential fact seems to be that the holiday enterprises have always been very much a minority concern. The residential hotels of Barry are few and dispersed in such a way as makes it impossible for them to invoke that sense of fat jollity which you get from a string of luxury hotels. Any attempt to give Barry a spectacular new face would be hazardous and extraordinarily difficult.

Gwyn Thomas (1913-1981): A Welsh Eye

Let's go to Barry Island, Maggie Fach

Let's go to Barry Island, Maggie fach,
And give all the kids one day by the sea.
And sherbet and buns and paper hats,
And a rattling ride on the Figure Eight;
We'll have tea on the sands, and rides on the donkeys,
And sit in the evening with the folk of Cwm Rhondda,
Singing the sweet old hymns of Pantycelyn
When the sun goes down beyond the rocky islands.
Come on, Maggie fach, or the train will be gone
Then the kids will be howling at home all day,
Sticky with dirt and gooseberry jam.
Leave the washing alone for today, Maggie fach,
And put on your best and come out to the sun
And down to the holiday sea.
We'll carry the sandwiches in a big brown bag
And leave our troubles behind for a day
With the chickens and the big black tips
And the rival soup-kitchens, quarrelling like hell.
Come, Maggie fach, with a rose on your breast
And an old Welsh tune on your little red lips,
And we'll all sing together in the Cardiff train
Down to the holiday sea.

Idris Davies (1905-1953)

A Paradigmatic Experience

Lavernock was not only a place I used to go to, it was paradigmatic experience in time; it was a crystallisation of the always-irrecoverable past.

It was those early Sunday mornings in summer, still cool before the heat, and a press of families standing on the platform. at Llandaff North station waiting for a train that was already half full, and that would be packed to standing room only by the times it left Grangetown, two stops later. It was the 'Yankee comic' I had been bought at a newsagents for the journey – a 'Lash LaRue' perhaps, or a 'Pecos Bill'. Then, when the train finally reached the little station at Lavernock – two platforms and a cream picket fence at the edge of a hayfield – it was the halfmile walk down that country lane between the fields to reach the beach, the crowd now strung out, as on a pilgrimage.

This of course was the middle Fifties: the halcyon days before diesel trains, before Beeching. They were compartment trains, without corridors, and the seats had a dusty reek never encountered since. Above were luggage racks of netted cord, like hammocks, and a foxed mirror between those sempiternally sunny monochromes of Great Yarmouth or the Wye at Symonds Yat. To lower the window you tugged, and released, a leather belt like a razor strop; and when you thrust out your abruptly windblown head – only one of many infant heads along your side of the swaying train – you had to keep your eyes screwed up when looking front in case of specks of hot coal in the warm, blustery slipstream buffeting your face.

This was also a time when few members of the working class owned cars, which meant that other places on the coast – Llantwit Major or Ogmore or St Donat's say – were out of reach. The trains didn't go there, and it was too far to cycle. You might get to Llantwit or Ogmore once a year, on the back of the lorry in the 'Whitsun Treat'. But otherwise – if you lived in Cardiff, at least – you went unfailingly to Lavernock. People 'from the Valleys' (i.e. anywhere north of Tongwynlais) were rumoured to prefer Barry Island, however: overcrowded, crass, commercialised, expensive Barry. (The reasons for this were unknown, but had, presumably, to do with that general cultural benightedness and gullibility attributed by all city-dwellers to those who live in the hinterland. Actually, it was probably a matter of which local rail line you were on for the coast.)

Lavernock, in any case, was much more basic. True, there was the nautically-named 'Golden Hind', a members-only drinking club. But apart from this, when you came off the country road, it was just a dust-and-gravel pathway down among the trees, the exposed roots of which were shiny from decades of footsoles. Then there were a couple of white-painted wooden shacks; these were boarded up and empty for seven or eight months of the year, but in the summer they sold the usual necessities: icecreams, tin buckets and spades, rainbow-whorled rubber balls, pink candyfloss, more Yankee comics, sandwiches and teas (with large deposit against return of teapot, cups, spoon, tray, etc.). There were also a pair of vile, fly-murmurous 'toilets' – latrine-sheds that led, it was believed, directly into the rusty, half-buried sewage pipe that ran a little way down the upper part of the beach before disappearing into the sand, only to debouch, presumably, somewhere out in the Channel. In any case, I – and I assume, most people – rarely used this amenity. We would simply wade out for another swim instead, on the cynical, urban assumption – almost certainly correct – that it would all end up there anyway.

Duncan Bush: from 'The Sea, The Sea' an essay,
included in 'Poetry Wales : 25 years',
edited by Cary Archard

A Wonderful Place

What a wonderful place the bay was. It was the shape and colour of a croissant and its outstretched arms, tipped with barnacled rockpools, hugged to itself a slice of glistening sea full of livid white bodies from the mining valleys. Suntan oil, seaweed and cigarette smoke wafted up from the sands in a salty-sweet sizzle that also smelt of hot deckchairs and tiny paper flags on sand castles. Behind the sun-smitten promenade, huddled in tamarisks, a row of green beach huts banked up towards the tennis courts. Beyond that houses glittered amid the hunched trees and above that lay a sheep-cropped golf course.

Wiggly with excitement I sat on the café terrace eating my ice-cream. I could almost hear the glistening wet sand down by the tide line crying out for me to lattice it with waterways of a Babylonian complexity.

Sian peered down the beach with an amused smile: 'It's all very bourgeois isn't it.'

'Oh yes, that's right. Can we go on the sands now?'

She sighed: 'How I wish I was in France or Italy now. They know how to visit the coast in style. My French penpal spends most of the summer walking on the Promenade des Anglais in Nice. She likes to sit and drink cappuccinos in the cafés there. Next year, I'm going to go over and spend the summer with her.'

'Bugger the south of France sweety – paradise, that's what you've got here mun, flipping paradise.' This intrusion emanated from a huge, sprawling miner who was roasting himself in a deckchair a few feet away.

Sian rolled her eyes: 'You wouldn't get this in Nice. Come on, we've got things to do.'

As I trailed behind her up the sandy steps to the promenade, the miner cupped a whisper in his hand: 'You know what I mean don't you,' he said, pretending to hug the sunshine: 'We love it.'

'Can we go on the beach now,' I said, when we'd strolled up and down the promenade three times. 'The tide will be in soon.'

'How tiresome you are. Let's sit down. People-watching, that's the thing to do when you come to the coast. Going on the beach is so childish.'

I wanted to say 'But, I am a child', but then I thought of my stiff new grammar school uniform hanging in a warm cupboard in an empty, sunlit house in the London suburbs; the house tie; the rugby boots; the new life. These were my last few days of wearing short trousers. A reluctant new member of the club of men, I sat on the wall, trying to hide my bucket and spade, the totems of my former self.

Richard Rhydderch: A Visit To The Bay,
a short story (2004)
Planet 167 Oct/Nov 2004

Cardiff

Here where the Taff ebbs its sort of one-man sea
Between the walls of a vein with no love of the black
                                        haemorrhage
There is a taste of despair, bridges of traffic to everywhere
Not reaching any, and all the wet past
Not belonging to the future. Here the Taff ebbs.

And I, as a lad open to spirits,
Language happened to me as a world occurs.
It dripped on me, took possession like a healthy ocean,

Formed waves around me and swelled an easy shoulder,
And yet fresh, pure, clear as water,
And drowned me.
There is something not recognized in water.
It is air that's heavier but without the distance of air
Be it on the edge of a lake like a white limb, in a mist of breath
Or on the bank of a brook, its stars a fairground without
                                                    sobriety,
Or the sea, the sea is a swan that moves
Across the sad bosom of our eyes without pining,
Moving with the power and the thickness of silence.

Water extends our meaning: it is the joiner,
The surround of our feeling, deep to the lip:
In baptism it is tranquil as a maiden's sleep
Touching our dry foreheads with knowledge of pain.
It comes into our hands like an animal;
It slips from our grasp like a life. But it is a spirit,
A spirit that's cold on legs. The earth's shirt.
The restless laughter of seashore nights.

When I was a lad in body, the Welsh language
That once splashed through the fun and majesty of courts,
But now sucks the meaning of our remnants together,
It was. How to word the beating of the heart?
The receiving on my forehead? It guided me
From hard streets, through corridors of clerks,
Foul their envy' and their self-conceit of bricks,
Along pound notes and nice lusts
To a bay. Oh how to tell of the kick of my eyes
On seeing the difference between what I was
And the chance to be whole as I had not dreamed of being?

Yes, water that scurries down to the roots is blood,
Collecting, a pool by holes of sap. It freshens
Clay soil that has had only hot-beaked hardship.
It is round, red as an apple. And Oh it runs
Among rushes like a girl, like a squirrel between the banks.
You'd laugh if you saw how babyishly
It clings to pebbles, its nose and its feet
And its tiny' hands groping. It throws
Arms around joy; the drops dance
On heads like locks of hair quicker than reeling rays.

With the leaden rain in the pure evening,
With the heavy water along this ground
The language falls word by word before the wrinkled wind,
Leaf-drops in the mist. Mist.
The standards have fallen, and now the words,
Red, yellow, brown, white, whirl towards the ground
To lie, how long, before they are rotten powder.

Here where the Taff ebbs its sort of one-man sea
The water retreats, swirling, sour sludge
And a stagnant pool. Will there be anything further
                              anywhere here?
A raw dry plain? Crumpled leaves
Without blue depth? . . . If so, let us rejoice
For the water that is left here; and not hoard.
Cheers, good luck, to God who has been moving
On the face of the waters. Cheers to Him
Who would raise living waters from a nation's well.

Bobi Jones
translated by Joseph P. Clancy

Tiger Bay

I watched the coloured seamen in the morning mist,
Slouching along the damp brown street,
Cursing and laughing in the dismal dawn.
The sea had grumbled through the night,
Small yellow lights had flickered far and near,
Huge chains clattered on the ice-cold quays,
And daylight had seemed a hundred years away . . .
But slowly the long cold night retreated
Behind the cranes and masts and funnels,
The sea-signals wailed beyond the harbour
And seabirds came suddenly out of the mist.
And six coloured seamen came slouching along
With the laughter of the Levant in their eyes
And contempt in their tapering hands.
Their coffee was waiting in some smoke-laden den,
With smooth yellow dice on the unswept table,
And behind the dirty green window
No lazy dream of Africa or Arabia or India,
Nor any dreary dockland morning
Would mar one minute for them.

Idris Davies (1905-1953)

Foghorns

When Catrin was a small child
She thought the foghorn moaning
Far out at sea was the sad
Solitary voice of the moon
Journeying to England.
She heard it warn 'Moon, Moon',
As it worked the Channel, trading
Weather like rags and bones.

Tonight, after the still sun
And the silent heat, as haze
Became rain and weighed glistening
In brimful leaves, and the last bus
Splashes and fades with a soft
Wave-sound, the foghorns moan, moon-
Lonely and the dry lawns drink.
This dimmed moon, calling still,
Hauls sea-rags through the streets.

Gillian Clarke

Dock

Greek and Irish, the shy Somalian
Make common language the city's nasal whine;
Brothers on the wharf as the cargoes
Come swinging overhead: oranges,
Iron, feldspar, grain, out of the sky
The worlds tangible gift, a pittance now

As a shadow shift works the freighters,
Alexandra Dock reproachful with echoes
And this south part of the city an empty hold.

In the chart shop maps like dust sheets hang
From drawing boards, and a last technician
Traces blue fathom lines, as delicate
As webs, the irregular shelving
Of a coast eight thousand miles away.
His pen unlocks the sea. It roars in my head.
The compasses stride a continent
From the white edge of its desert coast
To the equatorial heart; a vessel
Manoeuvres into green Bahia,
Its cabins a dizzying fug of languages.

'Walking the dock I find that world
Has vanished like a ship's brief wake.
Across the road the seaman's mission
Is a sour honeycomb of rooms
The walls of dormitories marbled by the damp.
But where the money came ashore
The banks are moored, ornate as galleons,
All dark Victorian mortar
And the sudden frosts of engraved glass,
Their sooted corbels thrusting like
The jaws of Exchange millionaires.
Straight down to the water's edge
The road runs like a keel.

Robert Minhinnick, from The Dinosaur Park

A Walk Around Butetown

A Somali taxidriver proudly pointed out to me a new mosque building for his community as he drove me from Cardiff station to the southern end of the nineteenth-century dockland once called Tiger Bay – the territory presumably perilous for landlubbers, not the tigers amphibious – and now reverted to the name of Butetown, after the Bute family which built the docks and grew rich on them. Here the city halts beside Cardiff Bay. Here the rivers Taff and Elan, coming down from the rugged, deeply-rutted coal-bearing area known as The Valleys, twenty miles or so north of the city, meet salt water. Here I intended to start my walk. Here, facing the brown mudflats of the Bay and the grey prospect of the Bristol Channel beyond, I put my backpack on a new bench, got Out my raincoat, and took note of my immediate surroundings. The former Pierhead Building still stood pre-eminent, a Victorian French Gothic concoction clad in terracotta, with hexagonal chimneys, gargoyles, and a castellated clocktower. Modern regeneration was signalled by newly planted bricks and cobbles, freshly painted black railings at the water's edge, and a bulky man in overalls crouching with a tape measure while a leaner colleague in jacket and tie jotted down figures.

I asked the latter official if there was a specific occasion for the fixing-up.

'One hundred and fiftieth anniversary of the docks,' he said. 'The railway came down here to the pier where the Campbell Line paddle-steamer ferries used to land. Fishing trawlers and Breton onion schooners went through the lock-gates into the West Bute Dock. That closed for ever in 1964. Now a few scrap-iron ships and dredgers use the last remaining docks. You wouldn't suspect it but at the turn of the century this was the busiest coal-exporting port in the world. There were ships out there, queued up halfway down the Bristol Channel, waiting to load Welsh coal.'

'And now?'

'Now we have plans for a barrage across the mouth of the Bay, constant high water within it, marinas, housing developments, thirty thousand new jobs over fifteen years. The legislation is coming before Parliament very soon. We'll get rid of all that mud. Where are you off to?'

I nodded northwards. I said, 'Up into the country,' judging it a bit early to confess to a stranger my ambition, which was to walk through Wales from bottom to top, from Bristol Channel to Menai Strait.

'You're in the right place to start. Bute Street goes up to the city centre. Keep right on for the main road, the A470, which will take you up into The Valleys. Good luck!'

I stood at the railings and took several substantial lungfuls of nutrient low-tide air. I looked at a small collection of ramshackle boats canted over at their moorings. I like mud. I wondered what the permanently raised water-level created by the barrage would do to the foundations and cellars of Cardiff houses, built on low-lying ground beside the Bay. I wondered how the Bay's waters, fed as they were by two unclean rivers, would be regenerated behind the barrage, walled off from the Channel tides. On the remains of the nearby ferry pier, a pair of railway-type semaphore signals – which had once controlled the berthing of ferry steamers – drooped forlornly. I began to walk: past a new Industrial and Maritime Museum, in whose yard a steam locomotive and a retired lifeboat, the Sir Watkin Wiiliams-Wynn, were parked. On the facade of the Pierhead Building, the same twin theme was struck in a plaque decorated with both ships and railway engines and in the motto of the railway company – *Wrth ddŵr a thân*, Through water and fire.

I sauntered slowly around this part of Butetown, past a

pub, still thriving, called The Packet, and a shop, with dusty, empty windows, which had last been a Merchant Navy haberdashers. A terrace of spruce-looking sandstone houses with Dutch gables facing out on the Bay had genteel net-curtained windows in which numerous small posters all chorused NO 'BARRAGE. The Bethel English Baptist Chapel had been re-named the Casablanca Club. The former Cardiff Coal Exchange building – which would have housed the Welsh Assembly if devolution had been approved in the 1970's – had become part of the empire of the barrage-promoting Cardiff Bay Redevelopment Corporation. The Mission for Sick Seamen was now a travel agency offering package tours by air to Tenerife. I paused at the gates to the surviving docks. NO ADMITTANCE EXCEPT ON BUSINESS said a sign, though within, across derelict land, it was hard to spot what business was going on in the distant warehouses.'

Anthony Bailey: A Walk Through Wales (1992)

In The Grip Of The Elements

A Canadian freighter, the *Anna Louise*, had gone aground over on the eastern side of Sveynton Bay, piling itself up on the Taskar Spur, a steeply shelving rocky peninsula which has been a hazard to shipping for centuries. As the tide ebbed, the water was rapidly leaving the Spur so that the full weight of the ship and its cargo was being borne by only a fraction of its keel and the ship was already beginning to break up when the call came for the lifeboat. There was confusion about messages, the telephone lines were blown down in a raging gale and the navy signaller who was supposed to have been aboard could not be found. But still, on my father's instructions, the lifeboat was launched and we all assembled along the cliff path to see the launch. Tom Grail was aboard, and seven good men and true with him, and I can remember the sea that night and the winking masthead light as the lifeboat entered the water and made its way across the Bay.

'Here on the Bristol Channel we see such seas on occasions that the factual descriptions detailing wave heights as given in official reports are inadequate. Wind forces too, are mere numbers unless you have the experience to match the figures, but on that night, I can remember staring out at the Bay as the sea retreated, dropping back and back, the moonlight exposing the violent shapes which the waves had made on the twisted seaweed torn from the rocks and strewn over the foreshore. Out on the Point, the westerly wind had whipped up the waves until they broke over the lighthouse itself, and round the corner, backsides, as we say, in the first of the little bays that extend down the coast, the waves lurched in a great rush, pounding down on the rocks in a succession of assaults, the white caps rippling and the hollows of the troughs deep and sucking behind, wind-blown spume blowing up in thick and eerie clusters right up to the road, and most frightening of all, the lurch of all that water on the back eddy seeming to scoop the pebbles away from the immediate shore as if the sea had determined it would have everything that moved that night. Men had been blown from motor cycles, a furniture van had overturned, the telephone lines were down, out in the channel the lightship had dragged her anchors, there was a street in the village without a roof left whole and as the maroons went, the first hazards which the running lifeboat-men faced were the flying slates from their own roofs.

And all the time, that westerly wind blew, howling down

on the Point from the great reaches of the Atlantic Ocean. Even when the sea retreated it did not lessen, but then, with the wind against the tide, the size of the waves doubled. You opened your mouth to speak, your spittle blew back in your face and the tears streamed from your eyes with the wind-whipped sand but this was an expected discomfort. As I stood, squinting out from the shelter of the Cutting, I could see the lights in the boathouse and I knew my father was in there, and there were still more men running along the pier as the late comers made their way to the boathouse, the wind blowing their hair, their raincoats flapping, heads bent to make headway. And all the time that wind howled and howled, a mean and unholy whine whipping through the broken telephone cables, sounding against the flapping corrugated iron sheets which had been torn from the pier buildings, whistling in the guttering of the cottage, the whole sounding in my ears like the wailing of all the demented souls that the sea had taken from us ever since the village had grown up in the shadow of the gallows far out on the Point.

Alun Richards (1929-2004): Ennal's Point

Flat Holm

Flat Holm – lighthouse, gulls, mist and rock. It's out there in the Bristol Channel in full view. Most Cardiffians have spent a life gazing but few have ever reached it. It's three miles in a straight line out from Lavernock point. Not far, but enough. Geographically it's the final extension of the Mendip hills that bump up through Somerset. Surprisingly it does not belong to Bristol, Avon, Barry or the Vale but is administratively a district of Cardiff County. Does the Lord Mayor know, I wonder. Does he drive across there in his Rolls? Unlikely. Flat Holm and its Cornish pastie near neighbour, Steep Holm, don't even have so much as a paved pathway between them.

Flat Holm is a mere 500 metres in diameter. It has three beaches, many rocky points and something called Dripping Cove. As its name implies, it's flat. It has none of the mystery of its steeper neighbour. The treasure or the shipwreck or the lost tribe will not be over the brow of the next hill. Stand in the centre of Flat Holm and you can see its entire world.

I come here in early September on the motor vessel 'Lewis Alexander', with thirty other visitors. The sea is as smooth as I can remember it. Flat, dull iron. No one is sick. Disembarking is a push over. There is a blackbird sitting at the top end of the jetty. Quite like home. Usually the island is the haunt of thousands of pairs of breeding gulls who feed off the rubbish tips of south Wales and fly back with their booty. The Warden keeps a collection of what comes back that's inedible – combs, hairspray bottles, bathplugs, empty Jif lemons, a joke rubber fried egg, the head of a toy dog, the leg from a doll. All carried by beak. Visitors are warned to wear a hat or hold a stick above their heads to ward off the defensive dive-bombing of the gulls. But September is not the breeding season. The birds are not at home.

Rosie, our guide from Fife, is a volunteer who's been here six months and whose accent is as impenetrable as that of someone from Llanystumdwy. She takes us from the farmhouse to the refurbished barracks and shows us the small Flat Holm museum. Here is a Neolithic axe head found during the excavation of the island's great treasure, the graves of the two murderers of Thomas à Becket. These last resting places can, of course, also be found elsewhere in Britain. But that's how it often is with the medieval world. Next to the axe head is a bulb taken from the Victorian lighthouse, a large key reputed to be from an earlier manifestation of the farmhouse (or even from the monastery that preceded it) and finally a small collection of books including Captain Marryat's sea adventures and the selected poems of Glamorgan's Professor of Poetry, Tony Curtis. Outside we discover Flat Holm's unique slow worm (it has a larger blue spot on its side than its mainland cousins), Flat Holm's unique wild peony (which also grows on Steep Holm), and Flat Holm's unique collection of wild leek (which also grow in Cornwall). These are Triffid-like and magnificent – four foot tall and with flower heads like giant rattles. At the centre of the island are the remains of a WW2 radar station. The whole of Flat Holm is littered with military left-overs. These go back through several centuries centering on the hardware generated by Palmerston's not entirely irrational fear that madman Napoleon the Third would actually invade. There are eighteenth-century cannon, earthwork emplacements and a defensive ditch which runs right across the island. This hollow is home to the marauding Alder, which is not officially classified as a tree, and the single Flat Holm horse chestnut, which is. This pathetic mid-channel example of the form, revered by Flat

Homers, looks pretty stunted and lifeless to me.

Peter Finch: Real Cardiff (2002)

Mighty Hills of Water

. . . into the sea, at one time or another, have gone sizeable chunks of Wales, for along this harsh western coast sea and land are constantly in tussle. Tales of catastrophic sea-floods, real or imaginary, haunt the Welsh folk-memory, and so many lives have been lost to the water that for centuries people in Gŵyr, the Gower Peninsula of Glamorgan, would never eat flat fish, those well-known scavengers of the drowned. Everywhere there are signs of the endless struggle. Sea-shore churches are choked with sand or wave-washed, like the unhappy church of Cwm-yr-Eglwys in Pembrokeshire, most of which fell into the sea during a Sunday evening service in 1859. Even towns and villages are threatened. On the southern coast huge sand-dunes have already obliterated the medieval borough of Kenfyg, with its church and castle, loom ominously through the woods outside the hamlet of Merthyr Mawr, and look poised to continue their advance over the M4 motorway towards the settlements of the interior.

A small metal plaque near the altar of Goldcliffe church, in the lowlands of Gwent, laconically records the most disastrous of historically recorded floods. At nine o'clock on a January morning in 1606 sea-waves came suddenly storming over the flatlands there, running 'with a swiftness so incredible, as that no greyhound could have escaped by running before them – huge and mighty hills of water', as the contemporary chronicler adds, 'tumbling over one another'. The whole coastal plain of Gwent was flooded, entire villages were swept away and 2,000 people were drowned, but this is how that plaque records the event:

> 1606. On the XX day of January
> even as it came to pass the flud
> did flow to the edge of this same
> brus and in this parish theare was
> lost 5000 and od pownds besides,
> XXII people was in this parish
> drown.

Today the Gwent flatlands shelter behind a long sea-wall, and the villages are safe (though even now their old buildings often have a washed-through, dried-out feel to them). Elsewhere around the coasts of Wales, however, are reminders of lands lost permanently to the sea – stumps of blackened trees revealed at low tide, islets where cattle used to graze, legends still current in guidebooks and pub talk about broken sea defences or inundated towns.

Jan Morris: 'Wales; Epic Views of a Small Country' (1998)

Severn Estuary ABC

A is a hat. Sun on my head.
B binoculars I'm using
C across the water. Largest concentration.
D is design. Planned.
E in Europe. Believe that.
F is mud flats, wading birds
C for godwit, green sandpiper, grey plover
H is heavy population, heavy water.
I'm informed. I watch tv. My hat is
Just there to stop the sun burning.
Know what does it?
L is little suns in bottles. Heat.
M is the mighty atom.
N for no trouble in Oldbury, Hinkley Point, Berkley
Old stuff, I know. They're not sure.
P soup of a public explanation.
Quantity before quality. The fuel of the future.
R is rich someone's salting somewhere. There's always someone
Severn seeped solid. Sold down the river.
T is truth. Piece of fiction.
Ah yes.
U is understanding. It's safe.
V is very safe. Formation of ducks. Skinhead. Thatcher.
We buy it.
X marks the spot. The insidious ingress. The cancer,
Why don't we do something?
Z is the sound of us listening.

Peter Finch

Mud

That first year I would come home to Newport for the weekend, and from the moment the train came out of the Severn Tunnel, from the second we entered Wales, I would be up out of my seat, at the door, waiting. I was that homesick for the mud. I'd stand at the door window for ten minutes watching the fields and hedgerows change into the furnaces and smoke of the steelworks, into the golf course, into rows and rows of washing lines and kitchen windows.

When the train finally pulled across the bridge I would pull and press down the door-window catch and hang my head out to feel the wind pinching my cheeks. I would close my eyes against the skewering rain and breathe in great big gasps of mud. The sweet-salt-sulphur stink of it.

Glorious.

I would pull and press down the door-window catch and lean my head out so I could see clear all the way down, over the bridge's rusted railings, down and down. All the way down to the Sainsbury's beacon sending its orange glow shooting out towards the opposite bank but only making it halfway before being pulled and pressed down, away into the mud.

I would jump onto the platform – always number two – when the train was still moving! so I could be the first off the train. The first to come home. The first to spin my tales of life in the big city, away from mud.

But I haven't been home for a while. Nine years, in fact. Been too busy. You know how it is. And I had to get rid of the mud. You don't stand a chance of making it in London if you're covered in mud.

Erica Woof: Mud Puppy (2002)

From 'Estuary Poems'

Under the stars they come ashore all night,
wading chest-high through the lights of Weston.
In the dark the current scoops and sleeks;
acres of scored mud plipping quietly.
See them flounder, waist-deep, long skirts dragging,
sick with the bilge-stink and hunger;
the river mocks them with its dangerous *croeso*,
the sucking pools, the children handed up,
lethal tidewash, wet caress,
fingers clutched in the soil and stones,
till the bank is firm and the land forms,
and they sit on the saltmarsh and slither into their shoes.

Cheaper than ballast, dumped in the dark.
Never uprooted from the memory's mud.

Catherine Fisher: 'Altered States' (1997)

Wreck of a Bristol trader

I Herbert Stevens of Whitson
will tell you of disaster
these Levels can never forget

in that storm a Bristol trader
smashed on Severn's channel shore
opposite Gwent's Nash lighthouse

I quickly collected neighbours
we rushed towards our landmark
struggled through mud as tide ebbed

one drowned sailor lay sprawled
on a newly exposed mudbank
four other roped to ship's mast
were also dead

              we stumbled back
carried them into Nash Church
for rest on the bellringers' floor

above us four boars' heads
stared from the tower parapet
that spire accused an absent God

Cornelius Cox of Church Farm
was expected to ring the bell
for evensong
              stood surrounded
by five corpses each movement
challenging death's stillness
every tone a passing bell

he took his place for service
bellringer among the living
followed ritual aware of
horror locked in that room
stunned we faced our future
knew tragedy blurred to history

Alison Bielski

Ode to the Severn Bridge

Two lands at last connected
Across the waters wide
And all the tolls collected
On the English side.

Harri Webb (1920-1994)